BOY POWER

How Famous Men Chose to Answer God's Call When They Were Young

Doris Irish Lacks

TEACH Services, Inc.
PUBLISHING
www.TEACHServices.com • (800) 367-1844

World rights reserved. This book or any portion thereof may not be copied or reproduced in any form or manner whatever, except as provided by law, without the written permission of the publisher, except by a reviewer who may quote brief passages in a review.

The author assumes full responsibility for the accuracy of all facts and quotations as cited in this book. The opinions expressed in this book are the author's personal views and interpretations, and do not necessarily reflect those of the publisher.

This book is provided with the understanding that the publisher is not engaged in giving spiritual, legal, medical, or other professional advice. If authoritative advice is needed, the reader should seek the counsel of a competent professional.

_____

Copyright © 2021 Doris Irish Lacks
Copyright © 2021 TEACH Services, Inc.
ISBN-13: 978-1-4796-1266-6 (Paperback)
ISBN-13: 978-1-4796-1267-3 (ePub)
Library of Congress Control Number: 2020915068

All Scripture used in this book is taken from the King James Version.

Published by

www.TEACHServices.com • (800) 367-1844

TABLE OF CONTENTS

Foreword . . . . *v*

Acknowledgements . . . . *vi*

1. Mountaintop Drama—Isaac 9
2. The Dreamer Boy—Joseph 15
3. The Escapee—Moses 19
4. Tell It Like It Is!—Samuel 23
5. Practice Makes Perfect—David 27
6. Little Boy—Big Decisions—Josiah 30
7. The Awesome Foursome—Daniel, Hananiah, Mishael, Azariah 35
8. The Calling—Jesus 38
9. Saving Uncle Paul—Paul's Nephew 41
10. Six Hundred Years Later—John Huss 45
11. He Changed the World—Johannes Gutenberg 48
12. The Boy Nobody Wanted—Leonardo da Vinci 51
13. Genius in a Hayfield—Isaac Newton 55
14. A Time for All Things—Johann Sebastian Bach 58
15. George Washington's "Rules of Civility"—George Washington 63
16. Super Talent—Wolfgang Amadeus Mozart 66

17. Friends for Life—William Clark and Meriwether Lewis 68

18. Decision on the High Seas—Joseph Bates. .71

19. From Invalid to Giant—John Byington 74

20. Log House to White House—Abraham Lincoln 77

21. The Miracle Worker—George Müller. 81

22. Pasteurized Milk—Louis Pasteur. 84

23. Boy Preacher—John Loughborough. 87

24. Ambition Personified—Thomas Edison 90

25. The Plant Inventor—Luther Burbank 92

26. The Man with an Engine Brain—Henry Ford. 95

27. Slave Boy to PhD—George Washington Carver 99

28. Working Together—Wilbur and Orville Wright 102

29. Little Red-Headed Monster—Winston Churchill. 107

30. Pigs to Watermelons—James Cash Penney 111

31. The Hardest Choice—Dietrich Bonhoeffer. 115

32. "Chimney Progress"—In the Bottom, Out the Top—Wernher von Braun . . 119

33. The Runner—Nelson Mandela. 123

34. Stubborn Winner—Desmond Doss 127

35. The Claustrophile—Isaac Asimov 131

36. I Have a Dream—Martin Luther King, Jr. 135

37. The Giant Step for Mankind—Neil Armstrong. 139

38. Beloved Soldier—Colin Powell. 143

39. Clean and Straight—Barry Black. 147

40. Conversion in a Bathroom—Ben Carson 151

41. Do it Right!—Bill Gates 155

FOREWORD

Are we spending so much time with our iPads, laptops, cell phones, and TVs that we don't have time to live? Are we caught up with constant news, sports, or entertainment that we forget our calling? Do we even know what our calling is?

God, our Creator, has given each of us abilities, interests, and talents that He's hoping we will use to assist others to encourage and help them in their struggles. What talents has He given you? You may answer, "Oh, I don't have any talents." Well, maybe you can't sing or play an instrument, but there are many more talents than that. What are the interests you have? Do you like machines? Art? Rocks? Bugs? Needle work? Building things? Math? Plants? Listening to and talking with people? There are so many kinds of talents! And everybody's different.

Most of the young men in the following stories had to go through hard experiences before they realized what their talents were, and that knowledge came about as they discovered what they wanted to do more than anything in the world. A few were chosen because God knew their potential before they did and before they decided to follow Him with faith and integrity.

Physical handicaps, even mental incapacities are overcome by some who use the abilities they possess to pursue a worthy goal and become successful through hard work and continual learning.

The ability to make right decisions comes from our Creator. He has a plan for your life. Just be patient and faithful in what's expected of you now, and it will come. Choice—what a source of power!

ACKNOWLEDGEMENTS

My greatest appreciation goes to Brian Strayer, Professor of English at Andrews University, who has for years labored through my work, correcting, questioning facts, and so kindly helping this "slow learner" to get published.

To all the experts at TEACH Services who make my amateurish writing publishable and who advertise so effectively.

To all my friends and relatives who have patiently listened to my enthused goings-on about what I'm writing at the time.

With all the billions of books out there, why do I have to write this one? Well, because the Lord has performed His miracles to encourage young people. He is still leading children and teenagers to overcome their love of ease, and to make this a better life for everyone.

1

MOUNTAINTOP DRAMA

1872 BC, Moriah

It was the middle of the night. Isaac, barely out of his teens, lay sleeping the untroubled sleep of innocence. Suddenly someone took hold of his shoulder and shook it. "Wha …? Who?"

"Sh-Sh." His father bent over him. "Don't make any noise. You'll wake up your mother."

Isaac sat up.

"What is it, Father?"

Abraham whispered, "God has spoken to me. He says I must go to a distant place to make an offering. We must start right away tonight. I need you to go with me. But don't wake up your mother."

Isaac, used to ready obedience, arose, dressed in his warmest clothes and silently went outside. His father had already summoned two servants who were loading a donkey with firewood and food. The four of them started out in the dark and headed northward. Toward morning Isaac noticed his father struggling to keep moving at the pace set by the younger men. As the sun rose, the face of his 120-year-old father showed signs of extreme anxiety.

"Are you all right, Father?" Isaac asked, coming closer to him.

"Oh, why, yes," he answered, emerging from deep concentration. The old man straightened and walked a little faster. Determination etched on his tired face.

Later, they stopped to eat the meal they had brought from home. Then they trudged on, sleeping for two nights in sheltered recesses and oases. Isaac awoke occasionally, hearing a voice and peering into the night. It was his father at a distance praying. Isaac had accompanied his father to worship God on many occasions, but somehow this trip was different. A premonition grew in his heart, but he couldn't resolve it.

On the third morning, Mt. Moriah came into view. A bright cloud covered the mountain's top. Abraham stopped and told the servants, "All right, here is where you stay with the donkey. Isaac and I will go up to the mountain and worship. We … we'll be back. Wait here."

The firewood was strapped to Isaac's back. Abraham took the knife and the small firepot and started toward the mountain. Isaac, knowing his father had not slept well for two nights, watched to see if he was going to make the rest of the trip to the top of the mountain, between two and three thousand feet in altitude. Abraham's face was a study in fear, sadness, and determination.

As they climbed, Isaac said, "Father?"

"Yes, Son."

"We have the wood, the knife, and the fire, but we don't have a lamb."

His father hesitated for a few moments before answering. His voice trembled. "The Lord will provide the lamb, my son."

Soon they reached the top of the mountain. Isaac knew from past trips that he was to gather rocks to build an altar. Together they placed the wood on top of the altar. "Now what do we do?" asked Isaac.

The moment had come. Abraham took Isaac's shoulders gently in his hands. "Isaac, first I want to tell you how much I love you."

"Why, yes, and I love you too," Isaac replied.

"Do you love God?"

"You know I do, Father. Why?"

"Do you trust Him?"

"I guess I do. Why are you asking me?"

Abraham said, "Do you remember the promise He made concerning you?"

"He said what you and Mother have talked about many times—that I would become the father of many nations."

"Do you believe it, Son?"

"Yes, I do."

"Even if you were to die today?"

Isaac looked into his father's face. "Father, what are you talking about?"

"God has told me that *you* must be the sacrifice."

"What?" The blood drained from Isaac's face.

"Yes, Son, you." Abraham's face contorted with sadness, and his eyes filled with tears.

"Father!"

"I know it doesn't make sense, but God told me. I've talked with Him enough in the past to know it was His voice."

"But, Father!"

Abraham covered his face with his hands, then looked at his son. "You remember the promise!"

Isaac by then was crying. "Yes, but …"

"I believe Him. That means that either He will resurrect you … or … or something. Do you believe Him? Do you trust Him?"

"I thought so. But why would He … ?"

"I don't know. Maybe He is testing us. I do know it was He that told me to sacrifice you. You can run away if you want to; I can't stop you."

Isaac looked around. Could he run back down the mountain, leave his father, evade the servants, … hide for the rest of his life? No! Where would he go? He couldn't hide from the God he loved and who loved him. He would just have to stay and do his part in the plan and trust God to do what He had promised. He looked down at the altar and replied, "I'll do it, Father."

Abraham burst into tears. Isaac's tears blended with his father's before the altar. They embraced and continued their preparation. Abraham tied Isaac's hands and lifted him up on the altar, his face to the sky.

"Do it quickly, Father," the boy cried.

He could see his father's hand with the knife raised in the air. He held his breath. Suddenly a voice like many waters called out, "Abraham! Abraham!"

"Yes, here I am!"

"Don't touch the boy. Now I know you trust Me. You have not withheld your son, your only son from me!"

The stunned silence that followed, as father and son heaved sighs of relief, was interrupted by a "Ba-a, Ba-a-h" in the bushes nearby.

"There's our lamb, Son!" Abraham exclaimed as he helped Isaac down and untied his hands. They embraced again, this time shedding tears of joy.

Centuries later God Himself offered His only Son, but there was no escape for Him.

Isaac
1892–1716 BC

"If any man will to do His will, he shall know of the doctrine ..."
(John 7:17).

2

THE DREAMER BOY

1728 BC, Canaan

"There you go, papa's darling."

It was a rough landing for the seventeen-year old. The well was empty except for some mud at the bottom. He regained his footing but was muddy from head to foot. It was cold down there. They had ripped off his coat.

"What have I done?" he shouted, his voice echoing against the walls of the pit. Hand dug and lined with stones, the well would be his home for some time. There was no way he could climb out. Had it been narrower, perhaps he could have stretched across with his feet and climbed up that way. But it was too wide. His brothers had abandoned him to this. He knew they didn't like him. At home he had tried to live right and make friends with them, but they had snubbed him and ignored him, and once in a while he heard them mimic him. That hurt the most.

And when he had dreams that seemed to put him above them, they mocked him. He dreamed that their sheaves of grain and those of his father and mother would bow down to his sheaf. He didn't know why he had such dreams. He learned quickly enough not to tell them what he had dreamed. Even his father was not pleased.

"Lord, what can I do?" he prayed. Praying was one thing that his parents had taught him and the other boys to do.

"Stay close to God, boys," his father had said, "and He will help you in bad times and good."

Just then Joseph heard voices above, voices of strangers talking with his brothers. "All right, then. Bring him up, and we'll take him." So, they let a rope down and hauled Joseph out. The strangers looked him over, mud and all. He looked into his brothers' faces. There was proud triumph written on some and doubt and shame on others. "Please! Please! Don't let them take me!" he begged.

"Sorry, little brother, you brought a good price, and we're going to have fun with it. And nobody's going to tell on us!"

His hands and feet were tied to the back of a camel, and the caravan started off. As they passed the fields of his home, he wanted to cry.

"Oh, Lord God, I'm a slave now! I might never see my folks again! What can I do? Will these people hurt me? Will I be able to escape? Am I going to die?"

As he rode along in the hot sun, he made up his mind. "Father God, I want you to know that no matter what happens to me, I will do my best to be true to You. I will try to do what they say and work as hard as I can. But please don't leave me."

The caravan traveled on for days, all the way to Egypt. There Joseph was sold again to an important government official. Later, unjustly accused of a crime, he served a long prison sentence. He dreamed dreams, interpreted the dreams of others, helped those in need, and became a trusted servant even behind bars. As a result, he was freed, promoted to Pharaoh's court, and was eventually instrumental in saving Egypt from starvation. In time, he would be reunited with his family.

You will want to read his story for yourself from the Bible. But, for now, let's just say that a boy's right decision ends up having a positive impact on many people.

Joseph
1745–1635 BC

"And we know that all things work together for good to them that love God, to them who are called according to his purpose."
(Romans 8:28)

3

THE ESCAPEE

1559 BC Raamses, Egypt

"Goodbye, my son," Amram said as he embraced his twelve-year-old son in his arms. "The God of heaven be with you always."

His mother and his older sister and brother likewise said their goodbyes, gave him parting advice, and expressed the hope that they would see him again. Their youngest family member was to leave home for a totally new life. From now on he was no longer to be a common Hebrew boy; he was on his way to being a prince. In fact, he might someday become pharaoh of the great empire of Egypt.

The boy stood straight and looked into the faces of his beloved family. "I hate to leave you, but I believe God has planned for me to help people. I don't know how He's going to do it, but I believe He's going to use me. I promise to stay true to Him." And all the others promised to stay true to God as well as they watched him climb into the royal chariot, stand by its driver, and disappear in a cloud of dust. He didn't see his mother cry.

At the palace, the princess, his adoptive mother, greeted him with hugs and kisses as she had done in years past when she would come to visit him while he lived with his family. "Now, my young man, come and see your new quarters." The sumptuousness of the suite took his breath away. His new wardrobe, large and elegant, awaited him.

"Your servants will help you get cleaned up and dressed," she instructed. "Then we will take you to meet your new grandfather, the pharaoh of Egypt."

They cut his hair and cleaned him up. Then they dressed him in his new military uniform, crisp, fresh, and colorful. He felt very much like an army general. "Ah, master! You look very handsome!" announced one of the servants.

The princess proudly took him into the throne room, and there sat the Pharaoh with his high headdress and pointed beard looking severe yet interested. "So, young man, you have come to live with us. I hope you will enjoy it. I expect you to learn our ways, our methods, and our discipline, and after you are thoroughly trained, you will make a great leader in this royal empire."

"Yes, majesty, I will do my best," he replied. And he did. He learned the Egyptian language, and he studied science, mathematics, literature, social life, and the religion of Egypt. More than anything else, he loved riding his handsome Arabian horse. He became the leader of the cavalry and a favorite with all his men. His godly patience and fair treatment toward all became a legend among the people, and all through his teens he stayed faithful to the God of the Hebrews. He never forgot the conviction that he was to be instrumental in helping his people. For the next few years, he proved himself capable and faithful in his responsibilities.

But suddenly, everything changed. One day, as supervisor on a construction project, he came upon an Egyptian beating a Hebrew worker. "Hey! What's going on?" he shouted. The beating continued, so Moses flashed his sword and killed the Egyptian. The Hebrew fled. Moses looked around, and since nobody was in sight, he quickly buried the dead body in the sand. His mind, trained in military conquest for years, told him, *You can do it, Moses. You can be the general of your people, and together you can conquer these Egyptians.*

But the next day everything changed. As he worked at the construction site, he saw two Hebrews fighting. "Hey! What's going on?"

They stopped and one replied, "So! Are you going to kill me like you killed the Egyptian yesterday?"

Moses, trying to keep calm, turned around and walked away. *They know! What am I going to do? As soon as Pharaoh finds out, I'm a dead man!* Reaching his residence, he gathered essentials together and strolled nonchalantly through the darkening streets to the edge of the city. By the time it was dark, and he was away from the city, he started to run. He chose a little-used path that soldiers would be unlikely to follow in searching for him. He ran for hours until he could run no more. He collapsed beside the path and burst into tears.

"Oh, God of my fathers! How could this happen? I've spoiled everything!" He wrapped himself in his cape as he'd been trained to do as a soldier, lay down, and fell into a troubled sleep.

Jump ahead forty years, and Moses has humbled himself before God, found a family in another country, and spent the time herding sheep. Now God is calling him to be a spokesman to the new pharaoh, and he is finally able to serve his people, setting them free. Yet, it took time and extreme circumstances for him to consent to doing things God's way instead of his own.

Moses
1571–1451 BC

> *"By faith Moses, when he became of age, refused to be called the son of Pharaoh's daughter, choosing rather to suffer affliction with the people of God than to enjoy the passing pleasures of sin."*
> (Hebrews 11:24, 25, NKJV)

4

TELL IT LIKE IT IS!

1159 BC, Shiloh

"Samuel! Samuel!" The twelve-year-old boy awoke with a start.

"That's master Eli calling me!" he said aloud, jumping out of bed and running through the darkness to where the aged high priest lay sleeping.

Samuel tried to awaken him by shaking his arm, "Sir, you called me?"

"Wha … oh … Samuel … what is it?" said the old man raising his white head.

"You called me, sir?"

"No, I didn't call you. You must have been dreaming. Go back to bed," Eli said lying back down.

So Samuel went back, climbed into his bed, and lay thinking. Then it came again, "Samuel! Samuel!" The boy jumped out of bed again and ran to Eli. "Father! Father! You *did* call me!"

Eli sat up, thought a few seconds and put his hand out. "Son, it was not I who called. Next time it happens, you say, 'Speak Lord, for your servant is listening.'"

Now back in bed, Samuel lay awake. Soon the voice came once again. "Samuel! Samuel!" Samuel sat up in bed and repeated the words Eli had told him to say. And God talked to Samuel.

God told Samuel things he didn't want to hear. "Eli's sons who hold sacred, priestly responsibilities here in the temple are dishonoring Me by the wicked acts they do here in My house, and their father knows nothing about it. But I know, and it's a shame. At first, I was sad, but now I'm angry."

"What do You want me to do?" Samuel asked.

"I want you to tell their father everything I have told you, and I know that you have seen some things yourself. Tell Eli all of it. It's time things changed."

The boy lay back down and thought to himself, *How can I tell Master everything I know? I've seen and heard a lot. He's not going to like it one bit. And if his sons find out I told him, what will they do to me? ... But God said I must tell Eli. I must obey. Maybe things will get better if I do.*

When Eli listened to the boy the next morning, his face turned pale in shock and sorrow, his hands shook, and tears came to his eyes, but Samuel told him everything. However, as time went on, nothing changed. Eli did not have the courage to rebuke his sons or to try to correct them. Neither did he remove them from their sacred office. So the Lord removed them His own way. They lost their lives in a battle with the Philistines.

Called to the duties of a prophet, Samuel learned early that a true prophet not only conveys God's messages about the future to encourage believers, but he relates God's rebukes and warnings even to the proud and unrepentant. Samuel remained faithful to that calling all his life, and God's people prospered because of that mission of love.

Samuel the Prophet
1171–1061 BC

"Obey my voice, and I will be your God, and ye shall be my people: and walk ye in all the ways that I have commanded you, that it may be well unto you. But they hearkened not ... I have even sent ... all my servants the prophets ... yet they hearkened not unto me."
(Jeremiah 7:23–26)

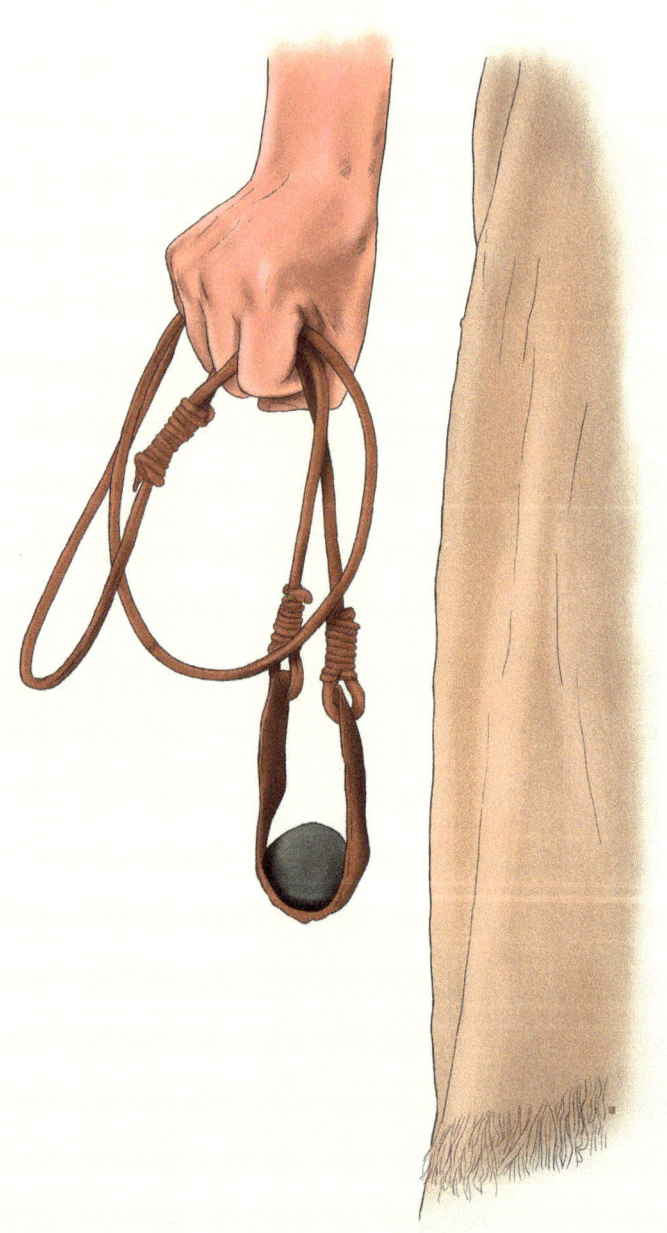

5

PRACTICE MAKES PERFECT

1063 BC, Bethlehem

The wilderness creatures trembled at the sound of a lion's threatening roar. The sheep raised their heads. The boy shepherd laid down his small stringed harp, set aside his writing materials, and stood up.

In a soft, gentle voice he spoke to his sheep, "Don't be afraid, my dears, I'll take care of you."

The lion crouched ready to spring toward the nearest sheep when a stone penetrated its forehead, and it fell dead. David's sling had done it again. Later that year, a bear met the same fate.

How could a stripling youth weighing not more than a hundred pounds kill a 300-pound lion and a 400-pound bear? Practice, practice, and more practice. Out in nature he had time without anyone around to distract him from learning and doing.

How can being alone teach a person to live right? Nature teaches many things—cause and effect, the power of right versus wrong, of music and poetry, and of love and truth.

"I'm determined to shoot with a sling," he had told his mother months before.

"That's good, Son. I've taught you to read and write, and I must say, you do it well."

"And you taught me mathematics which I'm not too good at, but I'll get better. I'm going to write more, learn to play the harp, and get better at slinging stones from the brook."

Mother asked, "What do you use as a target?"

"Well, I put a stone on top of a big rock and see if I can knock it off."

"I hope you don't hit any of your sheep."

"Oh, Mother, I wouldn't do that! My sheep trust me."

One day one of his brothers came to find him. "The prophet Samuel is here and wants to see you."

"Me? Why me?"

"He's looking for a certain kind of person. He says God is to tell him when he's found the right one. He's looked at all of us in the family, and we're not what he wants. You go home, and I'll watch your sheep."

When David stepped into the presence of Samuel the prophet, the old man's eyes lit up. "Yes! This is the one!" He turned to the family and said, "I know for certain that the Lord has appointed this young man to one day become the king of Israel!"

Everyone gasped. David shrank from Samuel. "Me? But I'm ..."

Samuel stretched out his arms to David. "You don't know how such a thing could happen, my boy, but God knows what He's doing. And He has told me to anoint you king right here and now!"

"But ... but ..." David protested.

Samuel took out a vial from his coat. "Here, Son, stand still and bow your head." God's servant poured oil over David's head. David sank to the ground, kneeling with everyone else. His knees were buckling anyway.

Years later, this shepherd boy did become king after many learning experiences in spite of the mistakes he made because he never lost his humble, repentant attitude and his determination to stay close to God no matter what.

David the Shepherd King
1078–1015 BC

"For ye see your calling, brethren, how that not many wise men after the flesh, not many mighty, not many noble, are called: but God hath chosen the foolish things of the world to confound the wise; and God hath chosen the weak things of the world to confound the things which are mighty." (1 Corinthians 1:26, 27)

6

LITTLE BOY—BIG DECISIONS

634 BC, Jerusalem

The boy's bedroom door opened, and his young mother entered quickly sobbing. She bolted the door and leaned her forehead against it, her shoulders heaving. After a few minutes, she turned toward her sleeping son and fell on her knees against his bed trembling.

"Ma … Mama?" he murmured, waking to her touch.

"It's all right, Son. Go back to sleep." He turned over and was soon asleep. But it wasn't all right. The eight-year-old had not heard the commotion downstairs. Mother Jedidah had seen the servants rush into the living room. They had not been called by her husband, King Amon. Knives flashed, and suddenly her husband was dead. She had run terrified out of the room and up the stairs. And now she lay herself under the covers beside her son. She still shook, and breathing came hard. Would they try to kill her too?

Oh, Lord God of my fathers, she prayed silently, *Oh, it was so awful! You saw it all. I have to trust You. I love You, but I don't understand. You know what kind of a man he was—cruel to so many, devoted to his gods, careless, and neglectful of me and his little boy. He even tried to put him through the fire to the false god Molech. Lord, I know my husband was a wicked man,*

6. LITTLE BOY—BIG DECISIONS

but I tried to love him. And now he's dead, wicked as he was, like his father, Manasseh. Our little son loved him. Why couldn't he see that and mend his ways? Please tell me what to do, Lord, as You have so many times in the past.

Her hands had stopped trembling, and she relaxed a little, but sleep did not come easily. The next morning, a gentle knock at the door brought her around. Little Josiah awakened.

"Who is it?" she asked.

"It's Hilkiah. Are you all right?"

"Yes, we're all right," she got up, unlocked the door and opened it.

Josiah bounced out of bed and greeted Hilkiah with open arms. "Uncle!" Hilkiah was not his uncle, but there had always been a strong bond between them. Hilkiah lifted him up and held him while he looked deep into Jedidah's eyes, "It's all over, everything is cleaned up. You can come down now."

That was the beginning of a new day in the life of little Josiah, and a new day for the whole nation. The eight-year-old was crowned king of Judah. Gone were the fears and hopelessness that the good people of the land had carried in their hearts for so long. Now the young ruler would have wise counselors as well as a godly mother to direct him in right paths.

When Josiah was sixteen, he said to his mother, "I have come to a decision."

When Josiah was sixteen, he said to his mother, "I have come to a decision."

"What is that, Son?"

"I have decided that I must take greater responsibility for the good of my people. I have talked it over with the God of heaven. I wish to give myself fully to Him."

"Oh, your friends the elders will be so happy to hear that because there are still a lot of enemies in the land, and with your help, things will get better."

And they did get better. After another few years, Josiah sent out workers to destroy the statues, idols, and images that many in the land bowed down to and worshipped. King Solomon, who hundreds of years before had built the magnificent temple but who later became careless and married many pagan wives, had erected heathen idols to please them.

Josiah took a personal part in the destruction of those huge images that could be seen above the trees on the mountain opposite the sacred temple. He broke them down and had them ground to powder and strewn across the water. He destroyed the idols that his grandfather, wicked King Manasseh, had put in the sacred temple, which was built and dedicated to honor God only.

Then, later, while builders renovated the neglected temple under his direction, the sacred rolls, were found gathering dust. These were parts of the book of Deuteronomy, which Moses had written under God's instruction many years before.

"Read it to me!" the King asked Shaphan, the scribe. Upon hearing the holy words, Josiah stared into space and then began to cry. He fell to his knees, bowed with his face to the ground, "Oh, Lord God, how wicked we have been! How ungrateful! How miserable we have been to dishonor You like this!"

As a result, a proclamation for all citizens to come together was made—to hear the word of the Lord. Then a great change came over the people. "We have sinned against our Maker. He is a merciful God. Let us live our lives in a way that will please and honor God and our beloved King Josiah!"

And they did.

King Josiah

642-611 BC

"Out of the mouth of babes and sucklings hast thou ordained strength because of thine enemies, that thou mightest still the enemy and the avenger." (Psalm 8:2)

7

THE AWESOME FOURSOME

537 BC, Babylon

Several hungry lions looked him in the eye. He couldn't get away. The walls towered above him. This was the scene of death for all enemies of the state. Usually such victims never reached the ground, but Daniel had, and the huge cats just sat there and looked at him. He concluded that he was going to spend the night in this place under the protection of the Creator of these animals.

But he couldn't sleep, of course. That would be presumptuous. Instead, he decided to think of the many ways God had led him through the years. He remembered when he was a teenager and part of the royal family during the destruction of their capital Jerusalem by the Chaldeans. He and several of his friends had been taken captive and forced to make the journey by foot to Babylon.

He remembered their conversations as they struggled along, tied together by the wrists.

"What do you think they're going to do with us?" he had asked.

His closest friends, Hananiah, Mishael and Azariah, looked down at their tired, dusty feet, sighed, and shook their heads. "It's anybody's guess," replied Mishael.

"Maybe they're going to kill us with great ceremony. Our folks back home died without a chance even to say goodbye." Azariah's face showed the shock and heartbreak he had experienced during the last few days since the destruction of Jerusalem and the death of his family.

"No, I think they are going to make us pagans like they are," suggested Hananiah.

"Well, we need to make some decisions now while we're on the way," said Daniel. "I say we should all think of how we are going to act, no matter what they do to us."

"Well, I can tell you right now, I'm not going to feel like cooperating with them one bit!" said Azariah. "They've been nothing but cruel—monstrous!—in their treatment of us and our people."

Mishael gazed into the desert sky. "In spite of all that, we're still alive. Maybe God has a plan in mind for us."

Daniel looked at his friends, sweat rolling off his face and back. "That's a good thought, Mish; tell us more."

"Well, maybe we could be kind of ambassadors—like they have between countries—and, though the Babylonians are our enemies, maybe God has something good planned. Being good examples of how to live right ... and ..."

"That's an encouraging thought," Hananiah called from farther back in the line. Daniel stopped and gathered the other three around him. "Quick! Let's pray that the Lord will lead us to honor Him in every way."

"Lord, we wish to represent You in everything we do and say, and even think. Protect us Father, Amen!"

"Here, you dogs! Get going!" shouted the guard on horseback. The boys resumed their 500-mile trek, but occasionally Daniel would look back, and the others would smile and nod their heads, "Yes!"

Magnificent Babylon, one of the wonders of the world, became their new home. They learned that they were to be educated into the culture of Babylon. Daniel remembered the contract with his three friends—that they would remain loyal to God and His principles, no matter how close the test.

In fact, he thought, *That's why I'm in this smelly lion's den.*

During his childhood he had been taught to be honest and hardworking and to honor God. A conspiracy among some of his enemies had resulted in this night with the lions, but now God was honoring him. He thought back a few months when his three friends had been thrown into a big fiery furnace for refusing to bow down and worship a statue the king had made, but they came out unharmed. They were honored by having the Son of God walk with them in the furnace. That gave him courage as he sat looking at the lions who were looking at him. The next morning the king commanded his release.

What tremendous power is available to us all!

Daniel the Prophet
607-584 BC (years of his captivity)

"Call upon me in the day of trouble: I will deliver thee, and thou shalt glorify me." (Psalm 50:15)

8

THE CALLING

AD 8, Jerusalem

"But where is he, Joseph?" Her lips quivered, tears filled her eyes, and fear etched her face. "He always stays with us when we get near home to help us unpack."

Our twelve-year-old Jehoshua was nowhere to be found.

"Maybe he's with my boys and their friends. Or maybe with our neighbors coming behind us," I suggested, knowing his mother would never be at peace until he was found.

I thought to myself, *I doubt very much that he's with my boys. They are a rowdy pair since their mother died years ago. There isn't much they won't get into. But they're reasonably decent to their stepmother. She's young and good to them, and she's trying to teach them in the right way. But I doubt her son is with them today.*

The donkey's hooves clip-clopped on the dry road, and the sun shone hot over us.

"I'm afraid," she said finally. "Let's turn back. We've got to find him."

I was thinking the same thing. *What if something really bad has happened to him?* I remembered when he was first born. We had to move quickly to another country to get away from that

What if something really bad has happened to him?

murderous fool of a king we had. As it was, before it was all over, the king had murdered hundreds of baby boys.

"He was such a good boy all the time we were at the festival," I assured her. "I'm sure he's back there behind us somewhere."

"Maybe he's already home," she said, then hesitated. "No, he wouldn't pass us up like that."

Some of our friends offered to take most of our belongings home with them so we wouldn't have to carry all of them back and forth. It was a good thing too. We walked back and met people we knew, but they hadn't seen him.

I kept thinking about how I depended on the little lad—now growing up—how he had helped me in my shop, how he made friends with all my customers, how he would sing when work got difficult or boring, and how he would sweep the floor and put away tools at the end of the day.

We went all the way back to the city. We looked everywhere—in the market, in the shops but with no luck. No one had seen him. My wife was exhausted from travel and worry—three days of it. So was I. Finally, we thought, *Could he be at the temple?* But why would he go back there? But—sure enough—that's where he was! And what do you think he was doing? He was sitting with the elders and teachers, talking about the Scriptures. He was asking them questions, and they were asking him questions. We heard him ask, "Why must the people follow rules that are made up and aren't even in the Scriptures?"

When he saw us, he was glad. He greeted us with hugs and introduced us to the men. They said, "What a fine son you have. In, fact, we think he's amazing. We would be happy to have him as a student in our school."

When we left, my wife quietly scolded him, "Son, why did you do this to us? We've been looking for you for days!"

He looked at her earnestly, "Why were you worried? Don't you know that I must be about my Father's business?"

And he wasn't talking about me. My wife's son is also the Son of God. I know you will find that hard to understand. None of us understands.

We just know it's true. His name Jehoshua, or "Jesus," means "Savior." He is called "Emmanuel" which means "God with Us."

Jesus
4 BC–AD 27

"For God so loved the world, that he gave his only begotten Son, that whosoever believeth in him should not perish, but have everlasting life." (John 3:16)

9

SAVING UNCLE PAUL

AD 60, Jerusalem

"We've got to get rid of him somehow!" growled one of a large group of men gathered together in a house in old Jerusalem.

"That's the only way we can save our religion. He's ruined too many of our people already," said another with hatred written on his face.

"Some say he's turning the world upside down, and I believe it," added another.

"For myself, I've decided to make a vow that I'm not going to eat anything until he's gone," said another, his hands tight fisted. "Do you want to join me?"

"There's power in numbers," replied the first, "Yes, we'll do it too. We won't eat or drink until the rascal is dead!" They all agreed, nodding their heads. The look on their faces and the tone of their voices spelled trouble.

"I have an idea," offered one of them. "Let's talk to our priests and tell them what we've vowed to do and have them get in touch with the Roman captain holding Paul in the palace for protection. Have them tell him that we have more questions about his beliefs, and when Paul comes near to talk with us, we'll kill him."

"Good idea!" they all chimed in. "Let's do it!"

As they got up to leave, they didn't notice a young boy sitting in the room playing a game by himself, nor did they notice that he had been listening to every word. The boy was thinking, *They want to kill Uncle Paul! But I love that man! He hasn't done anything wrong. He's given mother and me true words from Scripture. I can't let this happen!*

Rushing toward the office of the security guard, he thought, *But what if they find out I told on them? Maybe they'll kill me too.*

He stopped dead.

I'll stay out of their sight … and if I don't tell anybody except the officer, I know God will take care of me, no matter what.

Determination filled his heart and mind, and he hurried on to the prison to visit Uncle Paul, the famous evangelist who had won many Jewish people to Christ. The boy told Paul what the men were planning, and Paul told him to go tell the captain of the guard.

> *But what if they find out I told on them? Maybe they'll kill me too.*

At the guard headquarters, the officer showed surprise when a young boy came in and insisted on speaking to the captain right away. When the captain came out, he took the boy by the hand to a private place, "What is it, son?"

"You know the prisoner you have named Paul?"

"Yes."

"Well, there are some men who have told the priests to have you bring Paul down into a council as if they had something to ask him, but they have vowed to kill him as he is brought in."

"Is that right?" The captain thought for a few seconds, "Well, we'll see about that!"

The boy started to go, "I hope you can do something, sir. He hasn't done anything wrong. He's made a lot of people happy, and they're just jealous."

"I've heard quite a bit about him. Some like him; some hate him. I'll tell you what, young man, you've done a good thing. We're going to spoil the plans of those thugs. But one thing—I don't want you to say a word to anybody—I mean anybody! Do you understand?"

"Yes, sir!"

So the next day Paul's nephew learned that Paul had been taken away to safety in the middle of the night by 200 soldiers, 70 cavalrymen, and 200 spearmen. Thus Paul, the greatest evangelist in Christian history, was saved by a young boy who refused to be scared.

The Apostle Paul's Sister's Son

"But whoso hearkeneth unto me shall dwelt safely, and shall be quiet from fear of evil." (Proverbs 1:33)

10

SIX HUNDRED YEARS LATER

1386, Bohemia

As they trudged along a wagon trail toward the city of Prague, a mother and her teen-age son John talked. The widowed mother squinted toward the distant city. "I know you will do well, Son; you've proved yourself in school at home. Your father would be proud of you."

John shifted his pack to the other shoulder. "I hope so. It's not going to be easy, but I'm eager to start. The money will come. I can work, and I can sing."

Mother stopped. "Let's rest here under these trees. I'd like to pray before we get too close to the city."

> *We don't know where the money will come from, but please provide as You have since his father has been gone.*

John and his mother were used to praying together, so he laid down his pack and knelt with her in the grass in the shade. "Dear Father in Heaven," she began, "You know all about John. You know about all the people he's going to meet at the university—some good, some not so good. You have led him and protected him so far, but—please—by Your powerful Holy Spirit, help him to make the right choices. We don't know where the money will come from, but please provide as You have since his father has been gone. Thank You for John's faith in You, and may it grow until he becomes a faithful servant of Yours and brings many souls into Your kingdom. In Jesus' name, Amen."

John reached over and took her in his arms. "Thank you, Mother. I'll do my very best. And don't you worry."

The University of Prague welcomed John and accepted him as a "charity scholar." He amazed his teachers with his hard work and blameless deportment. He graduated with honors, took more schooling, and became a priest in the Roman church. Then he became a professor and, in time, the rector, or president, of the university.

But that's not all. His mother's prayers were answered way beyond her expectations. God called him to serve as a forerunner of the Reformation. He began to study his Bible more thoroughly and found many things his church taught and practiced that contradicted God's Word. He set out to try to change those things.

As he taught the people what Jesus was like, they could see the difference between Jesus and the rich, colorfully bejeweled church leaders who taxed the people's small means to build elegant cathedrals and enrich themselves.

In time, John was called to answer for his teaching because people by the thousands agreed and followed him. His defense was simple: "Show me from the Bible where I'm wrong." Finally, after a year in a dark, damp dungeon where he nearly died, church leaders brought him out and accused him again. He claimed the Bible promise, "When you are brought before councils for your faith, do not use your own words, for I will talk for you" (Matthew 10:19, 20, paraphrase). His testimony amazed the churchmen. He talked as if he had studied in comfort for all that year!

Finally, since they could not answer his challenge, they excommunicated and defrocked him and led him to a martyr's death where he sang until he died. But the people who believed the Bible kept the faith, and now six hundred years later, in much of the world freedom reigns.

John Huss
1369–1415

"Wherefore come out from among them, and be ye separate ... and I will receive you." (2 Corinthians 6:17)

11

HE CHANGED THE WORLD

1411, Germany

Eleven-year-old Johannes rushed through the archbishop's door where his father, a goldsmith, sat making coins. "Father! They're coming!"

Father quickly gathered up his work and put it in a safe place. "Let's go get mother and get out of the city." The German craftsmen had determined to rid the city of Mainz of all the influential nobility.

> *"Mother! They're coming!"*

"Mother! They're coming!" Johannes called out.

Father hurried upstairs. "We don't have time to pack. Get your shoes and coat, and we'll go out the back alley!"

"But … but where will we go?" said Mother.

"I don't know. We just have to get out of the city. We can think later."

And so Johannes and his parents traveled by foot out into the country. Mother, who was now wearing her coat, stared into the distance. "Maybe we could go to my family in Erfurt—this is the right road!" And that's where they went, stopping for food and rest where they could. Their family welcomed them happily.

One morning after they had rested, Father said, "Son, now we must find work."

"I'm ready. What will we do?'

"Well, I've taught you quite a bit of what I know about metalworking … and you must continue your schooling here in Erfurt."

In those days, there were no printed books. Everything was handwritten. Only in China and the Far-East were there printed books, though they were rare and difficult to print because they used carved wooden blocks. Johannes said to himself, *There must be some way to write on paper other than by hand*.

It would be some years before Johannes could put all his ideas together. But, when he did, he used his knowledge of metal.

"What do you think, Father, if I melted several metals together to make an alloy, one heavy and pliable, one light to expand it and make it less expensive, and one to bind them together and make the alloy hard and durable?" Father looked over the stock of metals he had collected. "What do you have in mind?"

"Iron, tin, and antimony to harden it."

Father's eyes brightened. "Excellent!"

So began the invention of movable type. Johannes made 290 metal cubes, each with a letter, number or a character such as a comma or quotation mark, each formed by pouring his alloy into a mold he had carved himself. Then he made a press (similar to a grape press to make juice) and arranged the metal type into words, painting them with an oil-based ink he had invented. Then he put the cover down which had paper attached, pressed it hard, brought the cover up and the printed paper could be read easily! This was how the first printed Bible, called the Gutenberg Bible, was produced, and there have been millions of books since. Now computer-run presses turn out thousands of pages an hour. What a different world!

Johannes Gutenberg
1400–1468

"So then faith cometh by hearing, and hearing by the word of God.... Yes verily, their sound went into all the earth, and their words unto the ends of the world." (Romans 10:17, 18)

12

THE BOY NOBODY WANTED

1452, Vinci, Italy

The little Italian peasant girl had just given birth to her first baby, but she was not happy. When they brought him to her, she turned her face away and would have nothing to do with him. She did not have a husband. The baby's father was a successful businessman in the town of Vinci, and he didn't want the child either. What to do?

Finally, the father's mother, a farmer's wife, offered, "Oh, I suppose we could take him home with us. We can't do much, but he can roam around with the cows and goats." So the child that nobody wanted started life on a poor man's farm. There was another man on the farm, an older son, who, when the child was old enough to walk, said, "Come on, Leonardo, let's go for a walk and see what we can find." So away they went.

> *So the child that nobody wanted started life on a poor man's farm.*

When the boy saw a bright colored bird, he pointed his little finger and shouted, "Unca! Ook!" even before he could talk well. Then he took out a scrap of paper and a stub of pencil and drew the bird.

"Well, look at that!" exclaimed Uncle, "You can draw a bird better than I can, and you're just a little tyke! We're going home to show this to Grandpa and Grandma!"

Grandpa said one day, "You know what we should do? We should ask your brother in town to bring some paper. I know paper is expensive, but the least he can do for his son is to get him what he needs. Then he can draw all he wants, and maybe he could learn to write." So Leonardo started taking a notebook on his walks and drawing pictures on the way.

When he was twelve, his collection of pictures was so good that his father came around and said, "Son, I can see you like art. Would you like to go to an artist's school?"

"Oh, yes, Father! Please! When can I start?"

"Soon, I think. But it's hard work. Are you willing to work harder than you've ever worked before?"

"Oh, yes! I'll do anything they tell me to do, and I'll do my best. I'll even do the things that I see need to be done!"

Leonardo was accepted into the school under a very good teacher, and he received the best training. The students even learned to make their own tools—paint brushes out of animal fur with wooden handles—and to make their own paint out of metals, plants, and insects. They were responsible for keeping the studio and themselves clean and for working well together. They learned how to carve, sculpt, paint pictures of people, make ornaments from gold and silver, and make pottery.

After a few years, Leonardo not only became an expert in the arts, but he also became an engineer and an architect. He even invented war machines for princes, dukes, and kings. He collected books on many subjects and read them eagerly. He became an athlete and a musician. Even though he failed often, he never gave up. He is credited with painting world-famous pictures, such as "The Last Supper" and "The Mona Lisa." No artist has accomplished as much as the boy that nobody wanted. The twelve-year-old boy who grabbed the chance to develop the talents God had given him grew from nothing into international fame!

Leonardo da Vinci
1452–1519

"When my father and my mother forsake me, then the Lord wilt take me up." (Psalms 27:10)

13

GENIUS IN A HAYFIELD

1660, England

A carriage approached the old farmhouse. The horse snorted as the reins tightened, and the carriage pulled up to the front porch. A woman came out wiping her hands with her apron. "Good morning!" called a well-dressed gentleman as he climbed out of the carriage and came to the front steps. "Are you Isaac's mother?"

"Why, yes. Did you come to see Isaac? He's out working in the field back there," she said as she pointed to the back of the farm.

"Well, yes, I want to see him, but I need to talk to you first."

"Please do come in. I'll fix you some tea."

As the two sat in the parlor, he began, "I'm the headmaster at Isaac's school, and I came to see you about the possibility of your allowing Isaac to return to school."

"Oh, no! I couldn't do that! I need him here. My husband, his stepfather, died about two years ago, and I asked Isaac to come home. I have to keep the farm going."

"Yes, ma'am, but have you ever considered any alternatives?"

After a few minutes of thought she said, "Well, I do have other children. They might think about taking over the farm. I'm getting on in years."

The professor replied, "I'm sure your children would help you all they can. I know Isaac would. But you need to know that Isaac has a mind that goes higher and deeper than anyone we at school have ever heard of!"

"Is that so?" Mother looked at him intently then down at her careworn hands.

The professor continued, "His ability to solve the most complicated mathematical problems so easily and quickly takes the breath away from every one of our faculty, and we all think it's a terrible waste for him to be out there cutting hay. I say this, ma'am, with all due respect."

"Well, I ... I suppose you're right. Let me call him in and see what he has to say."

Soon eighteen-year-old Isaac hastily cleaned up and entered the parlor. He shook hands with the professor. "What's all this about?" he asked.

Mother answered, "The folks at your school think you're too smart to be a farmer."

The headmaster interjected. "Oh no, don't get me wrong, ma'am. It takes a lot of hard work and figuring about what the weather and the government are going to do next to be a good farmer, but we think Isaac is beyond even that and that he can be an influence to improve our country and maybe the whole world."

And he was. Isaac Newton went on to school, graduated with honors, and entered Cambridge University. He became one of history's greatest mathematicians, scientists, government servants, and thinkers. He discovered and taught the laws of gravity, geometry, calculus, the effect of light on colors, magnetism, the science of motion, and other aspects of science. He became Chancellor of the Exchequer in England, changing the monetary system from silver to the gold standard. He prosecuted many counterfeiters. He never married, but he studied his Bible every day. He died at age 85, possibly from the high amount of mercury in his system from all his experiments.

Sir Isaac Newton
1642–1727

"Study to shew thyself approved unto God, a workman that needeth not to be ashamed, rightly dividing the word of truth." (2 Timothy 2:15)

14

A TIME FOR ALL THINGS

1696, Germany

The full moon shone brightly in the window. It was after midnight. An eleven-year old boy sat at a table writing. All was quiet in the house; his brother and family were sound asleep upstairs. What was he writing? He was copying some music he had taken from his brother's music studio.

> *"It's too hard for you, Sebastian. There are other things you need to learn first."*

It was some organ music he had wanted to learn, but his brother, who was teaching him, wouldn't let him play it. "It's too hard for you, Sebastian. There are other things you need to learn first."

His parents had died a few months before, so his older brother had taken him into his own home. It was a good family. The brothers came from a long line of German musicians—composers, singers, violinists, harpsichordists, organists, and they were all named "Johann," though they were all called by their middle name. Sebastian wanted more than anything in the world to be the best organist of all musicians. He was so eager that he determined to have that score even if he had to copy it in the moonlight.

One morning Christopher's wife said to him, "I can't get Sebastian up again this morning." Another morning she reported, "Sebastian is too sick to get up this morning."

"You know, it's about once a month that he gets these spells," commented Christopher, "and it's always about the time of the full moon. Do you think he might be sneaking out to party or something?"

"Oh, no, he's too young for that," she replied.

"Well, I'm going to find out what the little rascal is doing."

So, on the next full moon, Christopher stayed up, hid himself in places around the house, and finally found the "little rascal" copying music. He shouted, "What's going on here? What are you doing?" Sebastian jumped, almost falling off his chair. Christopher grabbed the paper, looked at it and exclaimed, "Sebastian! You're copying the music I said you couldn't have!" The boy hung his head. "Now you go back to bed! We'll talk about this in the morning."

Sebastian had a hard time going to sleep that night. Finally, he thought to himself, *Maybe he's right. I must learn all the fundamentals first. God has given me a chance to learn. I need to respect that chance with honor. I need to mind my brother. He's a good teacher, and I shouldn't try to go ahead so fast.* Then he went to sleep.

So the boy practiced every chance he got and learned to play the organ well. Soon he was hired to play in church. What a way to make money—by doing what he loved most! He grew up and became engaged to a lovely girl, Maria Barbara. One day they were in the church when Sebastian said, "You have such a sweet voice. Will you sing while I play the organ for you?"

"Oh, I couldn't do that."

In those days, women were not allowed to sing in choirs or as soloists in church, but Sebastian coaxed her until she consented. How beautiful it sounded! But suddenly the church deacon burst through the door and shouted, "What is the meaning of this?"

As a result, Sebastian lost his job. But he kept playing and composing. The determination and genius of Johann Sebastian Bach resulted in more than a thousand compositions and his great fame as an organist. He once said, "I will compose nothing that cannot be played in church."

Johann Sebastian Bach
1685–1750

"Who then is willing to consecrate his service this day unto the Lord?" (1 Chronicles 29:5)

15

GEORGE WASHINGTON'S "RULES OF CIVILITY"

1747, Fredericksburg, Virginia

Before he was sixteen years old, George Washington copied down 110 "Rules of Civility and Decent Behavior in Company and Conversation" as an exercise in penmanship. Thus did Washington early learn the secret of gracious manners and apply them to his gentlemanly conduct. The "rules" cover ten pages in one of Washington's copybooks now at the Library of Congress in Washington, DC. Here are some of sixteen-year-old George Washington's rules.

1. Associate yourself with men of good quality if you esteem your own reputation; for 'tis better to be alone than in bad company.
2. Wear not your clothes, foul, ript or dusty, but see they be brushed once every day at least, and take heed that you approach not to any uncleanness.
3. Be not hasty to believe flying reports to the disparagement of any.
4. Shift not yourself in the sight of others nor gnaw your nails.
5. Treat with men at fit times about business and whisper not in the company of others.

6. Be not curious to know the affairs of others, neither approach those that speak in private.
7. Eat not in the streets nor in your house out of season.
8. Read no letters, books, or papers in company, but when there is a necessity of doing it, you must ask leave. Come not near the books or writings of another so as to read them unless desired or give your opinion of them unasked, also look not nigh when another is writing a letter.
9. If you cough, sneeze, sigh or yawn, do it not loud but privately; and speak not in your yawning, but put your handkerchief or hand before your face and turn aside.
10. Do not express joy before one sick or in pain, for that contrary passion will aggravate his misery.
11. Let your discourses with men of business be short and comprehensive.
12. Play not the peacock, looking everywhere about you to see if you will be well decked, if your shoes fit well, if your stockings sit neatly and clothes handsomely.
13. While you are talking, point not your finger at him of whom you discourse nor approach too near him to whom you talk, especially to his face.
14. Drink not nor talk with your mouth full, neither gaze about you while you are a drinking.
15. Let your recreations be manful, not sinful.
16. Turn not your back on others, especially in speaking. Jog not the table or desk on which another reads or writes; lean not upon anyone.
17. Keep your nails clean and short, also your hands and teeth clean yet without showing any great concern for them.
18. Think before you speak. Pronounce not imperfectly nor bring out your words too hastily, but orderly and distinctly.
19. In visiting the sick, do not presently play the physician if you be not knowing therein.
20. Be not forward but friendly and courteous; the first to salute, hear and answer, and be not pensive when it is a time to converse.

21. Undertake not what you cannot perform, but be careful to keep your promises.
22. Speak not evil of the absent for it is unjust.
23. In company of your betters, be not longer eating than they are.
24. If others talk at table, be attentive but talk not with food in your mouth.
25. When you speak of God or His attributes, let it be seriously and with reverence.
26. Honor and obey your natural parents although they are poor.

George Washington
1732–1799

"Charity [love] suffereth long, and is kind; charity envieth not; charity vaunteth not itself, is not puffed up, doth not behave itself unseemly, seeketh not her own, is not easily provoked, thinketh no evil ..." (1 Corinthians 13:4, 5)

16
SUPER TALENT

1762, Vienna, Austria

Onto the stage in the royal palace walked a six-year-old boy dressed in silk stockings and a fitted velvet jacket with puffed sleeves. The musical conductor made the introduction to the royal family, to important friends in government, even to the composer of the evening's special music. The boy approached the conductor who bent down to hear his whispering. Then the boy looked out into the audience.

"Our guest has a special request to make," announced the conductor. "Would Master _____, the composer of the concerto we will be playing tonight, be willing to turn the pages for him?"

A man in the audience stood up, and the people began clapping in his honor. "Certainly," he said as he made his way to the stage. The old man and the boy sat down side by side on the harpsichord bench.

When all was ready, the conductor raised his baton, and the music began. The harpsichord strummed out with melody, chords, runs, and

> *The composer sitting next to him turning pages could scarcely contain his emotion, and tears trickled down his cheeks.*

changes of key. Like a veteran musician who had practiced and performed for many years, the little boy played his instrument. The composer sitting next to him turning pages could scarcely contain his emotion, and tears trickled down his cheeks.

The stringed ensemble had a hard time keeping track of their measures as they watched this young genius perform. At the end, the audience clapped, stood up, and shouted acclaim while Wolfgang bowed several times and left the stage.

This boy had been given such talent by his Maker that at age four he could identify blindfolded any note and any key in which a piece of music was played and could also identify chords. By age seven, he had written a sonata, and, by age eight, he had written a symphony.

Once he took the place of an absent second violinist in a stringed quartet, and, when the piece of music ended, the other musicians commented on how well he had done on a piece he had never seen before. Wolfgang responded, "Why does anyone who plays *second* violin need to practice?"

As the years went by, he composed so much music that he is lauded as one of the most prolific composers in history. He also remained faithful to God who gifted him with incredible talent!

Wolfgang Amadeus Mozart
1756–1791

As a postscript to our story, Mozart became very ill, was bedridden, and died suddenly at the age of thirty-five.

> *"The Lord gave, and the Lord hath taken away; blessed be the name of the Lord."* (Job 1:21)

17
FRIENDS FOR LIFE

1781, Fredericksburg, Virginia

The cave echoed with a splash, gurgle, and a terrified cry—"Will!" Water threatened to prevent any more calls from seven-year old Merne as he thrashed around in a dark pool. He had slipped off a ledge and lost his torch. He came up with another blubbering cry. "Will!"

Will thought to himself as he hurried toward his friend, *I should have followed him closer*.

"Here, Merne, take this rope and wind it around your wrist!"

With much struggle the two boys reached a level place and lay down exhausted, with Will's light still glowing in the darkness.

"Shall we go home?" Will asked.

"Oh, yes. I'm c-c-cold."

Will took off Merne's jacket and put his own over Merne's wet shirt. It was bigger than Merne's jacket, as Will was big for his age at eleven, but Merne appreciated the little bit of warmth, even if the sleeves were too long.

"You saved my life, Will!"

As they headed out of the cave into the warm sunshine, Merne said, "Whew! I thought I was a gonner!" He paused, looked at Will, and said, "You saved my life, Will!"

"Aw, it was nothing," replied Will. He stopped and looked ahead. "It was nothing—compared to facing your mother when we get home!"

The two boys from Virginia spent much time together hiking in the woods and talking of their dream of going west to see what was on the other side of the mountains. Once when Will was looking in books to find a map so he could copy it and give it to his father for his birthday, Merne said, "Will, when we go west, you can make maps of where we go!"

And that's exactly what happened. When Merne, who years later became Captain Meriwether Lewis of the Continental Army, was asked by President Thomas Jefferson to lead an expedition into the newly acquired Louisiana Territory from the Mississippi River to the Rocky Mountains and beyond to the Pacific Ocean, he accepted the challenge. And who do you think he appointed as his co-captain? Lieutenant William Clark of the Army. But Merne insisted he be called "Captain" too.

Will's job was to recruit strong, talented, experienced workers and sailors. Merne took charge of buying the best equipment available, a chronometer, a sextant, cooking equipment, and tools. He also got new boats built and more.

President Jefferson had medals made with his picture on them along with other gifts for the Indians. He also requested that plant and animal specimens be gathered along the way.

The expedition started in 1804, from St. Louis, Missouri, and proceeded into uncharted territory where few white men had ventured. They were the first white men to cross the Continental Divide. They faced hostile natives, cold, stormy weather, rapids, rocky rivers, sickness, and exhaustion all the way to the Pacific Ocean. But they did it! It took them two years to make it there and back. Only one man died, and that was from appendicitis. When they came back, they had more than a hundred maps and many plant and animal specimens that were totally unknown to the white man.

These two men who followed God's calling to explore the United States made their decision when they were young boys. What power there is in an early decision!

William Clark
1770–1838
Meriwether Lewis
1774–1809

"Again, I say unto you, That if two of you shall agree on earth as touching any thing that they shall ask, it shall be done for them of my father which is in heaven. For where two or three are gathered together in my name, there am I in the midst of them." (Matthew 18:19, 20)

18

DECISION ON THE HIGH SEAS

1809, Atlantic Ocean

"Are you all right, Heimy?"

Joseph helped his friend from beneath some barrels that had fallen over in the hold of the ship as a violent storm increased in fury by the minute. The boys thought they would be warm and protected under the deck, but when water began leaking in through a crack in the hull, seventeen-year-old Joseph said, "Maybe we'd better go up on deck. It's wet and slippery, but it might be better than staying down here."

Unfortunately, when they tried to open the hatch, it wouldn't budge. They tried again, but again it refused to open. Meanwhile the water on the floor kept rising, first covering their feet, then their knees. Heimy began pounding on the door, but no one heard. Joseph yelled as loud as he could and banged on the hatch too. But who would hear them with the wind howling and the waves splashing torrents of water over the deck?

It suddenly dawned on them that death could be near. They held on to each other, trying to keep themselves from falling into the water which by now had reached their waists.

Joseph prayed, "God, if you can hear me, please save us. I know I've never been close to you, but if you would give me another chance, I promise that I will live for you, and I'll try to do everything you want me to do. I know you're in control!"

Soon their knocking was heard above the howling of the wind and the lashing of the waves, and the hatch was opened for them. Freedom felt good even on the slippery deck with the sea pouring in.

After the storm, Joseph did not forget his promise. The Holy Spirit impressed him to get rid of liquor, tobacco, and other bad habits. And later, he began studying the Bible. Joseph often went to sea. As war broke out in 1812, United States President James Madison charged the British with violating America's sovereignty by restricting American trade with Europe, and he accused Britain of kidnapping Americans from their own ships to serve in the English navy. Joseph found himself in the middle of it all in Liverpool, England.

By now, Joseph was eighteen years of age. He and his friend were staying at a boarding house when burly members of an English press gang burst into their room and forced them out onto the street like criminals.

> "You can't do this to us! We're American citizens!"

"You can't do this to us! We're American citizens!"

"You just wait and see what we can and can't do," came a gruff voice behind him. Joseph could feel the sword at his back, and he could see the townspeople staring at him while making no attempt to rescue him and his friend.

"You can't force us to join your English navy, war or no war!"

"Don't be too sure of yourself," replied the lieutenant as they reached the river. The two men were dragged aboard a rowboat and carried to the "Princess" where they were imprisoned in the hold.

Joseph looked around at the men already there. "So, this is the way King George gets his sailors."

His friend replied, "There must be fifty or sixty of us here in one room!"

Upon asking around, they learned that most, if not all of them, were Americans who had been impressed by England to help in her war with France. Nobody's passport helped. Men from every walk of life—doctors, teachers, vacationers—all became sailors in the Royal Navy overnight.

England, along with Prussia (Germany), Belgium, Russia, and other European nations had fought against France's Napoleon Bonaparte for nearly ten years. Thousands of European men had lost their lives in the innumerable battles between 1805 and 1815 as a result of one man's satanic desire for power. It was five years before Joseph got home.

Years later, as the captain of his own ship, Joseph Bates allowed no smoking or drinking on board. The sailors found, after getting over the initial shock, that they could do better work under happier and healthier conditions.

Another thing Joseph discovered from his Bible study was that he should keep the seventh-day Sabbath. After retiring from the sea, he helped organize a Seventh-day Adventist Church in Jackson, Michigan, which is now the oldest Sabbath-keeping church in the world, as a part of a Christian denomination with over 20 million members. And to think that it all started down in the hold of a ship in a raging storm.

Captain Joseph Bates
1792-1872

"Remember the sabbath day, to keep it holy. Six days shalt thou labour and do all thy work. But the seventh day is the sabbath of the Lord thy God; in it thou shalt not do any work, thou, nor thy son, nor thy daughter, thy manservant, nor thy maidservant, nor thy cattle, nor thy stranger that is within thy gates. for in six days the Lord made heaven and earth, the sea, and all that in them is, and rested the seventh day; wherefore the Lord blessed the sabbath day and hallowed it." (Exodus 20:8–11)

19

FROM INVALID TO GIANT

1816, Vermont

Through wooded wilderness and rarely traveled wagon paths, eighteen-year-old John rode by horseback. The early 1800s saw this frail young man, sickly from childhood, not even able to go to school regularly or work on his father's farm for even a few hours a day, seeking something that would give him a feeling of value and a purpose in life.

"Ho there, Nancy, we'll get there soon enough." He reached a bony hand out to his horse's mane. Nancy's ears flipped back in response. The sun peeked through the leaves, telling John the day would soon end. They would stop for the night and sleep under the stars. The 45-mile trip would end tomorrow, and John would go to his first camp meeting. In fact, it would be his first approach to anything resembling Christianity. John and his friends were deists. They believed in a Creator God, but they did not believe in the divinity of Jesus. To them, it was up to humans to bring order out of chaos and to comfort themselves in the midst of suffering. A future life, in their minds, was doubtful. They took confidence in their beliefs from the fact that some of the country's founding fathers, like George Washington, Thomas Jefferson, and Ben Franklin, had been deists.

John's nine brothers and sisters were no help. They didn't seem to think about religion or even care. Mother was too busy. Father, who had become a Christian, spent some of his time on the Methodist preaching circuit calling on believers, instructing and encouraging them. He had suggested that John go hear the camp meeting speakers.

"You might find some relief from your sickness by getting away," his father said.

And it worked. John rode Nancy back home with a new attitude. "Jesus *is* God's Son, Nancy! He loves me! He died that I might live. I'm worth something, Nancy, and life is worth living! Nancy, do you hear me? He loves horses too!"

John went home, rid himself of his deist friends, and started studying the Bible and praying. In the months and years to follow, he experienced many ups and downs, but the Holy Spirit spoke to his conscience! "John, I have good plans for you. Don't give up. Keep going and growing."

John got a job on a fishing vessel off the Atlantic coast and regained his health. When he returned home to Vermont, everybody who saw him exclaimed, "John, is that really you? Why, you've grown so tall and straight, and tanned! And, man! Look at those muscles!"

John became a farmer and circuit-riding preacher. The time came when God, through His Word, convinced John to keep all the Ten Commandments. That included remembering the seventh-day Sabbath of the fourth commandment. He then joined other Sabbath-keeping pioneers to organize the Seventh-day Adventist Church. In fact, in 1863 he became the first president of the newly organized General Conference of Seventh-day Adventists, which has now grown from a few hundred members to almost 20 million today!

> *He loves me! He died that I might live.*

John Byington
1798-1887

"But as many as received him, to them gave he power to become the Sons of God, even to them that believe on his name." (John 1:12)

20

LOG HOUSE TO WHITE HOUSE

1825, Kentucky

"Get 'im, Scamp!" the ruffians shouted. "He thinks he's so smart. All that book larnin' ain't gonna help him now!"

The wrestling match between one of the strongest members of the group and the tall, lanky country boy looked to be one-sided.

"He doesn't even have any friends to help him!" shouted another. They all laughed. But, suddenly, the tall boy twisted his opponent into a hammer lock flat on the ground and pinned him down until Scamp conceded the match.

Abe proved his strength, developed by splitting logs with an axe at his country home. As he arrived home, his stepmother greeted him from the kitchen. "Abe, what happened to you? Your shirt is torn, and you look a mess!"

"Aw, some of the guys in town challenged me to a wrestling match. They said that, since I'm a bookworm, I don't know how to fight."

"Well, I bet you showed them, didn't you?" she said, taking two pies from the oven.

"I did. I don't think they'll bother me again."

"Well, you just keep reading and studying, and you'll make something of yourself someday, which is more than they'll ever do."

Abe eyed the pies. He loved his stepmother. She was kind and hard-working, and she always encouraged him.

"Ah, is that for supper?"

"It certainly is. By the time you get more wood in, get cleaned up, and the rest come in, we'll have supper."

In the years that followed, Abe grew to be 6'4" tall, and he educated himself in all kinds of subjects. His favorite reading, when not learning math, history, and grammar, was the Bible, *Pilgrim's Progress*, and books on literature and poetry.

He worked at various jobs, such as delivering products by boat down the Mississippi River to the southern states, and also as a shopkeeper and a postmaster.

Later he decided to become a lawyer, so he studied Blackstone's *Commentaries on the Laws of England* and other thick volumes of law. Even though self-educated, he passed the bar exam when he was 27 years old and went into business with a friend as an attorney. Then he decided to run for a government office, and from that time he became a politician. In traveling down the Mississippi to other states, he had witnessed the cruelty shown to slaves, and one of his greatest goals was to seek equality for all kinds of people, no matter what their race or color.

He became popular with the people because he spoke well to large audiences with reason and fairness, and, above all, he respected everyone—even his political enemies. Abe was later elected president of the United States. He suffered with his people through the Civil War and was often found in his office on his knees praying for strength and wisdom. He died in 1865 as the result of an assassin's bullet.

He is known for encouraging people to start manufacturing companies so they could sell their products instead of farming which kept them in poverty. He is known mostly for abolishing slavery and for keeping the United States united.

He said, "I will read and study, and some day my chance will come."

Abraham Lincoln
1809-1865

"If ye continue in my word, then are ye my disciples indeed. And ye shall know the truth and the truth shalt make you free."
(John 8:31, 32)

21
THE MIRACLE WORKER

1824, Prussia (pre-Germany)

"Hey, George, don'tcha wanna play another round?"

"Nah, I'm quittin' while I'm ahead," he replied as his clumsy hands gathered up his winnings. The room reeked with the odor of liquor where the boys had gambled all afternoon. Fourteen-year-old George stumbled as he made his way home.

"You're too late, George," murmured his father hunched over in his chair, his red tear-stained face lifting for a moment, "Where were you?"

> *"You're too late, George."*

"Oh, ah, ... I was helping Donnie's mother with her yard work."

"No, you weren't. Donnie's mother has been here all afternoon."

Caught in a lie again, George looked away. Father got up from his chair like a weary old man and faced his son, "We lost your mother this afternoon. She kept whispering your name until her last breath."

"Oh," was all George could say in his stupor. But in spite of his grief over losing his wife and watching George drinking, gambling, lying, and stealing (George even stole government money entrusted to his father), George's father decided to send him to a special school where he would learn to become a clergyman in the government church.

But school did not help George much. Then, one day, somebody invited him to a prayer meeting. There George heard for the first time in his life the story of Jesus, Emmanuel, God with Us—the Creator who offered to leave His place of honor in Heaven to come down to this sinful speck of a planet. He became a human being like us.

George learned that Jesus had lived a perfect, faultless life by His own choice and by His constant dependence on God His Father, but He was finally murdered by His own people, taking all the guilt of humanity upon Himself. But He came back to life again and stands in the courts above to help us and love us.

Crying, George went back to his room. He knelt down as he had once seen a man do, and he prayed, "Oh, God, how could I dishonor You with the wretched life I've been living?" That night George's life changed. In fact, overnight, the lies, the stealing, the gambling, and the drinking stopped.

The plan to become a comfortable government-paid clergyman disappeared too, and, instead, George became a real missionary. His prayer life produced unbelievable progress in his study of the Bible and in His giving of Bible studies and sermons.

He developed the goal of taking care of orphans, so he built an orphanage in Bristol, England. Then he added four more buildings. He is credited with providing a good home, clothing, and food for more than 10,000 orphans through the years. Not only that, but he also built 117 schools to educate 120,000 poor urchins in England so they could make a good living.

And you know what? He never asked anybody for a penny for all he did! He asked God to provide all that was needed. He kept accurate records of all that came in, and he returned a receipt for every gift he received, even if it was only a teaspoon!

George Müller
1810-1898

"Defend the poor and fatherless: do justice to the afflicted and needy. Deliver the poor and needy: rid them out of the hand of the wicked." (Psalm 82:3, 4)

22

PASTEURIZED MILK

1835, France

Father pushed his chair back from the kitchen table covered with schoolbooks and announced, "All right, Son, I've helped you evenings and summers for several years. I hoped that you could be a professor someday, but you don't have the same hope. God has given you talents, but you don't seem to care. I'm not going to help you anymore. You're in ninth grade now, old enough to do it on your own. It's time you took responsibility with your jobs here at home and ... well, it's your choice."

With that, Father left the room. Later, as Louis lay awake in bed, he pictured himself at school where his teachers indicated that they had given up on him too.

> *I don't want to be poor; I want to be a successful person. I guess I'd better change.*

Has everybody given up on me? What will become of me? I don't want to be poor; I want to be a successful person. I guess I'd better change. But I don't want to change.

Then he remembered what his father had said about God giving him talents. Had God given up on him too? He slipped out of bed and onto his knees as he had been taught from his earliest childhood.

"Dear God, please don't leave me. Please help me to want to get better. You know I don't like to work. So please help me to like it. I'll try …"

And he did try. Soon he began to like learning new things. He discovered how happy it made him to see his mother smile and thank him for his work around the house. And his grades began to improve. Soon he found a special interest in science—even more than his favorite hobby, drawing and painting. That decision in his bedroom changed his life. God had not left him.

Soon he graduated from school and then passed the entrance exams into college. He developed new traits of character. He took more challenging jobs. Soon he could pass difficult exams in chemistry and physics. After college he became a professor and a scientist.

He once wrote to his sister at home: "I beseech you again, work, love one another. Work … at first, I think it may bring boredom and tiredness, but once you have put your mind to it, you'll find that you cannot live without it."

Louis Pasteur became one of the most brilliant scientists in France and in the world. He discovered that a tiny organism called bacteria could kill a big cow. He discovered that if a healthy animal could be injected with weakened germs from a dead animal, that the healthy animal would not get sick. He is credited with saving France from total disaster from the anthrax disease that had killed thousands of cattle and sheep.

He discovered that the same treatment would save animals exposed to rabies. Then they brought him a nine-year-old boy who had been bitten by a rabid dog. Death—a terrible, agonizing death—was certain if he were to do nothing. With fear and trembling, Pasteur treated the boy, using his new method. He injected the boy with a weakened dose of rabies germs. For twelve days he gave him stronger doses, and the boy stayed well. By then, Louis knew the treatment was successful. The same method of inoculations with other diseases is used today.

How then did the little thick-headed schoolboy become France's most brilliant scientist? It was because he chose to use what talent God had given him and was not afraid of work!

Louis Pasteur

1822–1894

"Choose you this day whom ye will serve ... as for me and my house, we will serve the Lord." (Joshua 24:15)

23

BOY PREACHER

1848, Rochester, New York

Chills and fever racked the small, frail body of sixteen-year-old John. Barely five feet tall and 100 pounds, his work at the blacksmith shop making horseshoes and other heavy metal equipment had worn down his immune system to the point that he could not combat the malaria parasites that filled his bloodstream.

"Oh, Father in heaven," he pleaded, as he turned over in his sweat-dampened bed for the hundredth time and with another chill coming on. "Please! It's been two months since I've been sick. Please do something for me. Help me to get well or take me ... but, I don't want to die. I gave myself to You months ago. Have You forgotten? And my mother and everybody in the family have done so much for me, but they're all worn out." Then a thought came to him. *Maybe ...*

"Lord, do You want something? I've given You all I have—myself, my love. Yet, you've done so much for me—given me a home, a family, a job, the ability to build and make things, and the Bible, Your Word, and Jesus, Your Word made flesh. You have given me truth," he prayed, as he shook from the disease that had taken thousands of lives from New York to Panama. Mosquitoes were everywhere, wherever there was standing water. John continued, "Is there something You want me to do? Are You trying to tell me something? Do ... do You want me to win others to

You and to Your truth? Do ... do You want me to be a ... a ... preacher? A preacher ... a preacher! Yes, that's it! I'll be a preacher. I can do it! I'm good at public speaking in school. I love the Bible. I love people ... Yes! I'll do it. And I love You! Thank You God!"

John sat up in bed, looked around, turned, and put his feet on the floor. He shouted, "Mother! Mother!" He stood up, weak, but suddenly well, "Mother, I'm going to live, I'm going to live!"

And he did. He set out by himself, preparing Bible studies, sermons, and doing his own advertising, arranging meeting places in different towns. Friends helped him by giving him clothes, money, places to stay, and training. When people heard that a "boy preacher" was coming to town, they filled the halls to capacity. Not only did they come, but they learned Bible truths about Jesus' dying on the cross for all mankind, His soon coming, the state of the dead, the resurrection, and how to live a healthy, happy, secure life.

> *"Mother, I'm going to live, I'm going to live!"*

John lived to be 92 years old, still small but powerful. He became an ordained minister, serving in many capacities as an administrator and as a member of many boards and committees around the world, giving the wisdom of his years of experience and his dependence on God to the newly formed Seventh-day Adventist Church. He told adults and children delightful stories of his many travels, using the accent from each country, and he recorded others' stories too. He read the Bible through seventy-two times.

In spite of a life-threatening disease, his life was saved to win souls for the heavenly kingdom. God knows what He is doing.

John Loughborough
1832–1924

"If thou turn away thy foot from the sabbath, from doing thy pleasure on my holy day; and call the sabbath a delight … then shalt thou delight thyself in the Lord; and I will cause thee to ride upon the high places of the earth, … for the mouth of the Lord hath spoken it." (Isaiah 58:13, 14)

24

AMBITION PERSONIFIED

1859, Port Huron, Michigan

Tom stood on the platform at the depot with his pile of newspapers, waiting for the passenger train loaded with workers going into the city. It would be another ten minutes. But wait—here came a train now! The switchman must have made a mistake. The 2:00 freight train was supposed to be going south, but here it came!

Just then three-year-old Willie, son of the teletype operator inside, came out and ran onto the track. "Hey, Willie! Come back!" shouted Tom, dropping his papers. "Whoo-ooh!" whistled the train. It was coming too fast. Quick as a flash, Tom jumped out, caught Willie around the waist, and pulled him to safety just as the train roared by.

"Whew!" exclaimed Tom, as Willie's father burst out the door.

"Willie!" cried his father, falling to his knees and holding him close. He looked up at Tom with tears in his voice. "What happened?"

Tom explained, and the father replied, "He's always been so good to stay by me."

By this time Tom's passenger train was approaching, and even though Tom was still shaking, he gathered up his newspapers to sell to the passengers.

The next day Willie's father said to him, "My wife and I would like to reward you for saving our son. All the money in the world isn't enough." He pulled out some bills.

"Wait!" said Tom, "I've got a better idea. I've always wanted to learn teletype. Could you teach me?"

"Could I! I'll teach you everything I know, and for certain, you'll make a better operator than I ever was!"

So that is the way Tom Edison got started in his career. While he learned Morse Code, sending and receiving messages, he also learned how to receive the latest news from the National News Services, and he started printing his own newspaper, which his 300 customers loved. "From a thirteen-year-old boy? He'll go far," they said.

And he did. Even though he was the youngest of seven children and so unruly in the lower grades that his mother had to homeschool him, he finally learned to discipline himself. He decided to read everything he could get on certain subjects, especially electrical science. Eventually he became a full-time inventor.

Thomas Edison is honored today for having invented 1,093 successful devices, including the first successful lightbulb, the movie camera and projector, batteries, the phonograph, and a printer for the stock market. He is credited with being the most influential scientist and inventor in the 19th century.

One of his famous quotations is, "Opportunity is missed by most people because it's dressed in overalls and looks like work."

Thomas Edison
1847–1931

"Declare ye among the nations, and publish, and set up a standard; publish, and conceal not: say, Babylon is taken ... her idols are confounded, her images are broken in pieces." (Jeremiah 50:2)

25

THE PLANT INVENTOR

1859, Massachusetts

Luther walked through the fields on his father's farm searching for just the right daisies that he could plant in his own small garden.

When father saw them carefully planted, he stormed, "Luther! What are these weeds doing in your garden?"

"I planted them."

"You planted them? Why in the world would you plant weeds? They're a curse to us farmers!"

> *"Luther! What are these weeds doing in your garden?"*

Luther knelt beside his two weeds that he had dug up with his pocket knife so carefully and transplanted. "Well, I've noticed that no plant is exactly the same as any other, and, if you put pollen from one onto the center of another, you'll get seeds that will grow plants with some of the appearance of both. Then you pick out which of their children are the best and keep on planting 'til you get what you want. I want a big white daisy. It may take a long time but I'm going to keep trying."

Dad's eyes twinkled. "So you're going to scatter the bad ones around so we can have more weeds?"

"Oh, no, I'll burn them."

"Well, that's good. But it sounds like it's going to take a long time."

Luther stood up and straightened his shoulders.

"Someday I'm going to move to California where they have two or three growing seasons every year."

When he grew up, that is what he did. With more growing seasons his experiments developed faster. In the meantime, he invented a new kind of potato instead of the reddish potato everybody ate. One day he found a small green potato seed bag. Potatoes usually grow from cuttings with sprouts and seldom develop seeds, but Luther found a small green seed bag in his mother's garden. He guarded it carefully until the next planting season. The next fall he dug up his potatoes and found two hills that had white potatoes! After another planting season, more white potatoes grew. He sold his new hybrid to a plant nurseryman and saved the money to move to California. In fact, in the following years his new Burbank potatoes helped feed the people living in Europe who were starving because their potatoes had all developed a blight.

Luther worked for the next 55 years with thousands of experiments and invented seventy-eight new fruits, nine new vegetables, and eight new kinds of nuts. Also, from thirty-five different kinds of cactus plants that he had developed without spines or thorns, he was able to provide nutritious food for livestock, saving ranchers millions of dollars. He kept an accurate record of all his successes and failures. He was determined to help people around the world, and he did.

Have you seen those big, beautiful, pure white Shasta daisies growing in people's flower gardens now? They all came from his father's field of weeds! And most of the McDonald's french fries you love come from Burbank potatoes!

Luther Burbank
1849–1926

"The kingdom of God ... is like a grain of mustard seed, which ... is less than all the seeds ... but when it is sown, it groweth up, and becometh greater than all herbs, and shooteth out great branches; so that the fowls of the air may lodge under the shadow of it." (Mark 4:30–32)

26

THE MAN WITH
AN ENGINE BRAIN

1875, Dearborn, Michigan

"Dad! Look!" Twelve-year-old Henry pointed down the street, "What is that?!" Father, who had brought Henry to town to help him buy supplies for the farm, shaded his eyes with his hand.

"Well, it's some kind of a contraption. Let's take a closer look."

Henry, dressed in overalls, looked closer. "It's got a steam engine like a train, only smaller."

Father spoke to the driver. "Sir, how do you steer this thing?"

The inventor explained the simple workings of the first road vehicle Henry and his father had ever seen—and it changed Henry's life forever. "I'm going to make a machine like that, Dad—only better!"

"Well, there's plenty of work on the farm, but we'll see. Say! What time is it getting to be? We'd better get our things and get home. There are cows to milk."

Henry pulled out his pocket watch by its chain, "It's quarter to four. Yeah, Dad, thanks for this watch! I'm so proud of it."

But the next day, when Father entered the living room, there was Henry with his new watch spread all over the library table in parts.

"Henry! what have you done to your watch?"

"I'm seeing how it runs."

"You'll never get it put back together again!"

"Don't worry, Dad, I'll get it together again."

And he did. In fact, he began helping the neighbors with their watches. So, besides farming, Henry took to repairing clocks and watches. Then, every weekend, he would walk four miles into town to attend church.

Then tragedy struck. Henry's mother died. He and his father, brothers, and sisters were paralyzed with sorrow. They all agreed that "a farm is not a farm without a mother." "We're all going to have to work together," said Father, "And I expect you, Henry, to take charge."

But after a couple of years, Henry said to father, "Dad, would it be all right with you if I moved to town? I just can't do this anymore."

"It's all right, Son," said his Father. "You go get yourself an education, and we'll be all right." So Henry went to the big city, got a job with an electric company, took bookkeeping in college, and—wonder of wonders—he got married!

"Henry! what have you done to your watch?"

He married a girl from back home, one of the neighbor girls. So, when Henry was nineteen, he and his new wife moved back to the farm. Now he could work and make a living. He farmed, ran a sawmill, and began working on his first vehicle in a workshop that he set up in his barn. The first that he built was a tractor to help with the field crops, then he worked on his first car.

Deciding that a steam boiler was too dangerous, he developed a gas engine. His first horseless carriage had a carriage body with bicycle wheels, which he called his "quadricycle." He drove it ten to twenty miles-an-hour for maybe a thousand miles. Then, unlike other developers of road vehicles of that day, Henry sold his first car and used the money to build a second one, then a third, and that's the way the Ford Motor Company got started. Henry said, "I want to build my Model T so simple that everybody can own one."

Henry was the first to develop the factory assembly line where parts being assembled would move along on a conveyor belt, and each worker would do just one part of the job. He also started the first eight-hour workday, with his employees working around the clock in three eight-hour shifts. The cars came off the line so fast and so cheaply that even the factory workers could afford to buy a car! It is said that they were able to roll a car off the belt every 27 seconds!

Ford sold millions of Henry's Model T's all over the United States, Canada, and Great Britain. His automobiles changed American life forever.

Henry Ford
1863-1947

"Blessed are they that hear the word of God, and keep it." (Luke 11:28)

27

SLAVE BOY TO PhD

1890, Tuskegee, Alabama

"What are all these old bottles, jars, and pans for?" asked the college professor.

"I'm cleaning them to use for experiments. My students have brought them from junk piles all over town. I was invited to teach plant chemistry here, but I didn't have anything but tables and chairs, so we're starting small and simple," replied the new professor. "My students are anxious to learn how farmers and gardeners can grow crops without depleting the soil."

"Well, you're just the man to do it. I've heard you've been able to solve the problem in our cotton fields," replied his co-worker.

"Yes, cotton plants take a lot of nutrition from the soil and don't put anything back."

"How did you find that out?"

Professor George wiped out a bottle with a cloth and set it down in a row with his new "lab equipment."

"Oh, I've been around plants almost all my life. When I was a boy, I spent most of my time alone since my brother and I were the only black kids in the neighborhood and were not allowed to go to school. So I spent a lot of time out in the woods, pulling up all kinds of plants and replanting them in my garden. It was a secret garden. I learned which plants grew best in the sun and which ones liked the shade, and how much water each one needed to stay happy and growing."

"So how did you end up here?" asked the other teacher who had begun to help George with the bottles.

"My parents, who were slaves, had died, but my owner took me in, and his wife taught me how to read and write. I will always appreciate that they treated me and my brother like their own children." George stared into space remembering. "Mr. Carver even gave us his name, which I appreciated so much. And I read everything I could get my hands on—books, magazines, newspapers, the Bible. When I was ten years old, I moved into a home with another family where I did housework. I was too sickly to work in the fields. But there, my adopted mother taught me how to make medicines from herbs and wild plants. I was also able to go to school."

The two men sat down at one of the lab tables. The professor said, "This school wants good Christians for teachers; where did you learn about Christianity?"

"I was a mere boy when I converted, hardly ten years old. There isn't much of a story to it. God just came into my heart one afternoon while I was alone in the loft of our big barn shelling corn to carry to the mill to be ground into meal."

"How did that happen?"

"Well, a dear little white boy, one of our neighbors about my age, came by one Saturday morning, and in talking and playing, he told me he was going to Sunday School the next morning. I was eager to know what a Sunday School was. He said they sang hymns and prayed. I asked him what prayer was and what they said. I don't remember what he said, I only remember that as soon as he left, I climbed up in the loft by the barrel of corn and prayed as best I could. I don't remember what I said; I only recall that I felt so good that I prayed several times before I quit. My brother and I were the only colored children in that neighborhood. We were not allowed into a church or a Sunday School, or a school of any kind. That was my simple conversion and I have tried to keep the faith."

After his professor friend left, George sat thinking. In spite of all the feelings against colored people in those days, he was able later to go to school, to graduate from high school, get into college, and, with the help of his art teacher, get into an agricultural college in Ames, Iowa, where he earned his Bachelor's and Master's degrees.

The Eight Cardinal Virtues George Washington Carver taught his students are:

1. Be clean both inside and out.
2. Neither look up to the rich nor down on the poor.
3. Lose, if need be, without squealing.
4. Win without bragging.
5. Always be considerate of women, children, and old people.
6. Be too brave to lie.
7. Be too generous to cheat.
8. Take your share of the world and let others take theirs.

George Washington Carver received an honorary doctorate degree from Simpson College in 1928. He invented over 300 products from peanuts. He served as Professor of Agriculture at Tuskegee Institute for 47 years.

George Washington Carver
1864–1943

"And I saw another angel fly in the midst of heaven, having the everlasting gospel to preach unto them that dwell on the earth, and to every nation, and kindred, and tongue, and people, saying with a loud voice, Fear God, and give glory to him; for the hour of his judgement is come: and worship him that made heaven, and earth, and the sea, and the fountains of waters." (Revelation 14:6, 7)

28

WORKING TOGETHER

1886, Dayton, Ohio

"Hey!" the two brothers shouted, "Dad's home!"

Father, a church administrator who traveled the world, lugged his suitcase up the front porch steps. The boys rushed out to meet him with hugs and excited greetings. They grabbed his baggage and shouted to their mother, "Ma! Look who's here! See how tan he is!"

The whole family celebrated Father's homecoming with a special dinner prepared by Mother and the boys' sister, Katharine.

"Katharine," Mother said, "While the boys are upstairs helping Father unpack, would you please pick up the pieces of metal and wire the boys have been working on?"

"Oh, Mother, why do I have to pick up after those two? It's just trash anyway!"

"Never mind, dear. It's all right. Just put it away as neatly as you can on the shelf in the kitchen. They rushed out to meet Father. They'll get back to it later." Mother herself liked to build toys. She had even built a sled for the children that was every bit as good as one from the store.

Later that evening, Father entered the living room looking very mysterious, holding something cupped in his hands.

"Does anyone want to see what I'm holding?"

"Yes! What is it?" they all asked.

He opened his hands and out flew into the air a tiny toy like a bird. It hit the ceiling and fell to the floor. Both boys jumped up and picked it up, examining it carefully. "It's run by a rubber band!" exclaimed Orville.

"It's great!" agreed Wilbur. "Thanks, Dad, can we have it?"

"Absolutely. I thought you'd like it. I saw it in a shop in Paris and thought, *My boys would like this.*"

That night, as Orville and Wilbur lay in bed, Wilbur said, "Orv, I just know there's a way people can fly in a machine."

"I believe you're right. Shall we try to build one?"

"We already know something about how birds' wings are shaped, how they soar into the wind without flapping their wings. Why can't a machine do the same thing?" continued Wilbur.

"It's pretty dangerous business. Quite a few men have tried to fly with all kinds of get-ups, but it hasn't worked, and some of them have fallen and gotten hurt or killed," Orville warned, "but we should start small and simple and not be in too much of a hurry."

"Yes, we'll have to study the principles thoroughly, and that may take a while."

"Meanwhile, we'll have to make money in order to finance the thing," Orville added, "We don't want to be indebted to anybody, then we can be our own boss and make our own mistakes. But how are we going to do that?"

> *Quite a few men have tried to fly with all kinds of get-ups, but it hasn't worked, and some of them have fallen and gotten hurt or killed.*

"Well," replied Wilbur, "you know how everybody wants a bicycle nowadays. How about if we opened a bicycle shop?"

"Great! We could even make the bicycles!"

So the boys opened a bicycle shop. Bicycles were all the rage, and almost everyone rode a bicycle, even their sister Katharine and her girlfriends. Profits from the bicycle shop helped the boys finance their first glider. They had learned that birds cannot soar in a calm, so they concluded that they must take their glider where the wind blows constantly.

"I've found just the right place," exclaimed Wilbur after inquiring of the U.S. Weather Bureau. "It's on the coast of North Carolina. The sandy beach there is level, the wind blows all the time, and there's hardly anybody there." So they packed up their glider, and off to Kitty Hawk they went.

That began four years of successes and failures, added ideas, experiments, more research, using money from their bicycle shop. "We won't ask for any loans from the government or big corporations to finance this work," said Wilbur.

"Right," replied Orville, "Too much money has been lost by people who try to experiment with something they don't know anything about."

"Like us!" laughed Wilbur.

So the two young men continued to build, trying out their machines, riding into the wind, learning to turn around and land where they started. All of this was done while the news media either ignored them or laughed at them, drawing cartoons of them and saying, "Who wants to bet on their breaking their fool necks?"

But the day arrived in 1904 when the first engine-powered airplane circled around over Dayton with one of the Wright brothers high above a wondering crowd of spectators. And they had achieved it all by God's help, working together—not always agreeing—but working it through together.

"No bird can soar in a calm!"

28. WORKING TOGETHER

Wilbur Wright
1867–1912
Orville Wright
1871–1948

"Owe no man any thing." (Romans 13:8)

29

LITTLE RED-HEADED MONSTER

1882, England

"I won't!"

"Yes, you will!"

"You can't make me!"

"Oh, is that right? You see this paddle? It's going to change your mind, you stubborn imp!" With that the teacher gave Winnie the severest thrashing he ever got. Did that change his mind?

No. The red-headed freckle-faced boy refused to study Latin and math. He considered it a "waste of time" to study that which didn't interest him. Because his parents were so busy with their social life, they didn't have time to raise their son, and they left him in the care of his nurse. Winnie did well in history, though, and in English literature and grammar. He could memorize poetry like nobody else. The only reason he passed to the next grade was because his father was rich and influential in England and—let's be honest—his teachers were glad to get rid of him.

That's the way it was all through school. Winnie was always at the bottom of his class, even at age nineteen when he attended military school where it was the policy to put the worst students in the cavalry. But this delighted Winnie to no end. He said, "This is wonderful! I love horses. They're even going to give me a horse of my own!"

Soon he decided to make military science his specialty. Of course, that included a few subjects he had neglected before, and he studied diligently, including all the books he could get on military expertise. As a result, he graduated eighth from the top in a class of 150. With God's help, before too many years, he became a government worker, a military leader, a social reformer, and, eventually, the Prime Minister of the British Empire.

Winston Churchill is credited with inspiring the English people to work with faith and determination to keep their country free from Nazi oppression. He is also remembered for upholding free immigration for Jews ("Free entry and asylum for all"), for establishing the eight-hour workday, a minimum wage, workers' rights to have time off for meals, and government funding for unemployment insurance. He worked for prison reform, relaxing many unfair prison policies and establishing libraries in prisons. During the Second World War he encouraged the manufacture of tanks and steel helmets for troops and proper recognition of bravery in battle. He also encouraged leniency for Germany after their defeat and spoke against communism.

Here is a famous excerpt of a speech he gave during World War II.

"We shall go on to the end.

We shall fight in France,

We shall fight in the seas and oceans,

We shall fight with growing confidence

And growing strength in the air.

We shall defend our island

Whatever the cost may be."

Winston Churchill
1874–1965

"Behold, I have refined thee, but not with silver; I have chosen thee in the furnace of affliction." (Isaiah 48:10)

30

PIGS TO WATERMELONS

1883, Hamilton, Missouri

"But, Dad!"

"I'm sorry, Son, but the neighbors are complaining. Pigs make such a smelly mess."

Eight-year-old James had saved his money and bought a pig, fed it, and watched it grow fat. Then he sold it and used the money to buy some baby pigs. And there's nothing cuter than baby pigs.

"But, Dad, they're growing so fast, and they're so smart!"

But James had to get rid of his beloved pigs. He moped around for several days until he got a new idea. As he and his family were eating watermelon one evening, James exclaimed, "Hey, look at all these seeds we're spitting out. I could plant them and get lots of watermelons! I could clean out my pigpen, make a nice garden out of it, and grow lots of watermelons!"

And that's how James learned the fundamentals of business—good ideas, honest, hard work. He was hoping to earn enough money to go to college someday and become a lawyer.

But then his father, a Baptist minister, became very sick. As he grew weaker and his tuberculin cough increased, he called James to him. "Son, I'm not going to last too much longer, and you're going to have to help support the family. I've arranged for a job for you at the retail store in town. Would you do it?"

"Sure, Dad. I'll do the best I can." So James worked in town. After a few months, however, his own health began to deteriorate. He had caught his father's disease. The doctor said, "What I think you ought to do, James, is move to a place that's at a high altitude, in the mountains, maybe Colorado. I believe the cool, pure air will help you get well." And it did.

Later, James began to work in a retail store, part of a chain of three stores called The Golden Rule. The owners began to observe the honesty and salesmanship skills James possessed and offered him a third partnership with them. After a few years, when the owners decided to sell, James bought them out and named the new stores after his own name. He began adding more and more stores. Before long, the number of stores across the United States totaled 1,660!

When the great financial crash of October 1929 happened, the whole country experienced a terrible depression. James lost most of his money and had to borrow funds to pay his employees.

He worried himself sick and even contemplated suicide, as thousands of businessmen had done. Instead of giving in, he checked himself into Dr. John Harvey Kellogg's Sanitarium in Battle Creek, Michigan, which taught good health principles.

One morning he heard singing down the hall. He followed the sound and found the doctors and nurses having their morning worship. They were singing the song, "God Will Take Care of You."

> "Be not dismayed whate'er betide, God will take care of you;
> Beneath His wings of love abide, God will take care of you.
>
> Chorus:
> God will take of you, through every day, o'er all the way;
> He will take care of you, God will take care of you.

Through days of toil when your heart doth fail, God will take care of you;
When dangers fierce your path assail, God will take care of you.

All you may need He will provide, God will take care of you;
Nothing you ask will be denied, God will take care of you.

No matter what may be the test, God will take care of you;
Lean, weary one, upon His breast, God will take care of you."

That song saved James's life. He went on to become the head of one of the most successful chains of stores in the United States. It is said that he returned 10% tithe to the Lord and shared profits with his employees, helped with Boy Scouts, the YMCA, 4H clubs, and other youth organizations. His business grew—like watermelons!

James Cash Penney—J.C. Penney
1875-1971

"Bring ye all the tithes into the storehouse, … and prove me now herewith, saith the Lord of hosts, if I will not open to you the windows of heaven, and pour you out a blessing, that there shall not be room enough to receive it." (Malachi 3:10)

31

THE HARDEST CHOICE

1918, Germany

Making paper airplanes interested the boys in class more than what the teacher was saying. As one plane sailed across the room, the teacher thought to himself, *This is not working. What shall I do?* He laid his notebook on his desk and walked down the aisle and asked, "Harold, what do you want to be when you grow up?"

"Well, I don't want to be a teacher!"

Everyone laughed.

"I can understand why," the teacher replied, "but seriously, have you thought about it? What would you really like to be?"

"I want to be a pilot," Harold said.

"That's good, very good. And what about you, Victor?"

And on through the class, they talked about what they dreamed of doing.

"And Dietrich, what about you?"

"I'm going to be a theologian."

"A theologian?" The teacher smirked as the class laughed. "So, what is a theologian, in your opinion, my young man?"

Dietrich looked around embarrassed. Then his face took on an expression of confidence. "A theologian is a Bible scholar and … and …" But he couldn't put his feelings into words. All he knew was that the Bible stories his mother read to him at night excited him more than anything else. Being twelve years old, he didn't know if he could do it, but he did know that if God could lead David and Joseph—and Daniel—when they were young, He could lead him.

Their classroom was rather dark because Germans in the years between World War I and World War II lived in poverty. The schools, however, kept educating children to become scientists and doctors. Adolf Hitler was rising in power, and young men were being called into the military.

As Dietrich grew older, he studied hard, went to high school and college, and then to a university to study theology. "I don't want to go into the army," he told his best friend, Hans, a Jewish boy interested in marrying Dietrich's sister.

"Well, I'm planning to work for a company that delivers messages for the government. Why don't you do the same?"

So Dietrich and Hans avoided conscription and traveled. During that time, a conspiracy arose to kill Hitler, who had become a dictator and had convinced most Germans that his ideas and methods would restore Germany to world dominance. One of his ideas was to rid the world of all Jews. He had them gathered into concentration camps and gassed to death by the millions.

Both Dietrich and Hans were arrested for being part of the conspiracy and spent the rest of their lives in prison. Dietrich lost his life on the gallows just weeks before World War II ended. Hans died in prison.

Millions of brave people lost their lives during World War II. Dietrich Bonhoeffer had to choose between serving his country or the God he loved. He is remembered in hundreds of books, articles, movies, music, poems, and statues. He said, "Don't get on the wrong train because no matter how fast you run toward the back, you won't make it back home."

31. THE HARDEST CHOICE

Dietrich Bonhoeffer
1906–1945

"We glory in tribulations also: knowing that tribulation worketh patience; and patience, experience; and experience, hope." (Romans 5:3, 4)

32

"CHIMNEY PROGRESS"— IN THE BOTTOM, OUT THE TOP

1924, Germany

"I'm sorry, Mother," Wernher said as he handed over his report card.

"Why, Son! You've failed math again!"

"I just can't get it. Anyway, I don't like it."

"What about the other students in your class?"

"Oh, I guess they're all right."

That evening his dad looked over the report card. Dad was an important man in the German government. He set the card down and said, "What are we going to do with you?"

This situation continued for a few years until one day something happened that changed the boy's life. As a confirmation gift into the Lutheran church that he and his family attended, he received a telescope. With it he could see out into space.

"Dad! Look! See how the moon looks so close! And there are so many more stars than you've ever seen before!"

"Yes!" replied Dad peering through the new instrument. "There's the Milky Way!"

Later, when Wernher found a book in the school library entitled, *Rocket into Planetary Space,* by Hermann Oberth, a German scientist, he couldn't lay it down. He thought to himself, *That's what I want to do—find a way to get to the stars! But I could never be a scientist. Scientists are smart. I'm not smart ... Well, I guess I could be. Maybe if I could work harder at math ... and some of those other subjects like physics and algebra. Maybe I could do it. I've never worked really hard at studying ... but maybe I could. Yes, I could ... Yes, I can! I'll do it!* And he did. Within a few months, Wernher went to the top of his class.

At age eighteen, Wernher joined the Spaceflight Society, went to college, graduate school, and then earned a PhD in mechanical engineering, specializing in liquid-fueled rockets, which he helped send into the air two miles up. When World War II broke out, Wernher, a German, was expected to continue his work with rockets, which he did, though he was reluctant to use them to kill people. But the German government did it anyway. Near the end of the war, Wernher and his brother, Mangus, also a fellow rocket engineer, willingly surrendered to American Allied troops, saying later, "We knew we had created a new means of warfare, and the question as to what nation, to what victorious nation we were willing to entrust this brainchild of ours was a moral decision more than anything else. We wanted to see the world spared another conflict such as Germany had just been through, and we felt that only by surrendering such a weapon to people who are guided not by laws of materialism but by Christianity and humanity could such an assurance to the world be best secured."

> *Dad! Look! See how the moon looks so close!*

Wernher soon found himself in the United States, happy to become part of the national effort to put humans into space. He later became deputy administrator of the National Aeronautics and Space Administration (NASA).

32. "CHIMNEY PROGRESS"—IN THE BOTTOM, OUT THE TOP

Someone invited him to church where he expected a country club atmosphere, but instead, he found a small white frame building where the people were simple yet intelligent and they loved the Bible. There he experienced a true conversion. From then on, he grew strong in faith for the rest of his life.

He said, "The natural laws of the universe are so precise that we have no difficulty building a spaceship to fly to the moon and can time the flight with the precision of a fraction of a second. These laws must have been set by somebody.... The universe, as revealed through scientific inquiry, is the living witness that God has indeed been at work." He also said, "Anything as well-ordered and perfectly created as is our earth and universe must have a Maker, a master designer; there can be no other way."

Wernher von Braun
1912-1977

"And God saw every thing that he had made, and, behold, it was very good." (Genesis 1:31)

33

THE RUNNER

1923, South Africa

The family men sat around the room after dinner while the womenfolk ate their dinner and cleaned up the dishes and kitchen. Little Rolihlahla (translated "troublemaker") sat with them and listened.

Said one, "Our forefathers were so brave, and they never gave up their fight for the freedom they enjoyed at birth."

"Those Europeans came down here to South Africa thinking they could take over without a fight," said another, "but they were fooled."

Another elderly grandfather said, "And the fight goes on. Now they have taken away our citizenship. When is it going to stop?"

"Not until we get our freedom back."

"But we don't have the leadership we need," replied another.

Little Troublemaker listened, thinking, *Who do they think they are—taking away our country from us? When I grow up I'm going to fight for my people.* Years later, troublemaker, who was the first in his family to go to school because he was to be the tribal king someday, thought of freedom as he took his daily run. *I am grown up now, and I'm going to help end this separation. We've got to learn to live together.*

No longer was his name "Troublemaker." The good teacher in his church school gave him a Christian name—"Nelson." And Nelson finished school and went on to attend different colleges, with the goal of becoming an attorney. During those years, he participated in political demonstrations and was once expelled from school because of it. The tribal king was so angry over it, he called Nelson home and began searching for several wives for him to make him settle down to tribal life.

But Nelson escaped, ran away to another country, finished his college education, and organized the first black law firm in South Africa. He also spent those years doing all he could to end the racial separation. He participated in civil uprisings, wrote letters, and visited the leaders of other countries, asking for help to end the policy of apartheid (the African name for racial separation), until finally he was arrested and sentenced to life in prison. His enemies thought they had gotten rid of him, but he kept on writing letters and pamphlets to distribute. He used every means he could think of to unite the people of South Africa.

Finally, the political mood changed enough that the separation was ended. Nelson was released after twenty-seven years in prison. He eventually was greatly honored by receiving the Nobel Peace Prize, and he later became president of a free and democratic South Africa. One of his most famous quotations was, "I have fought against white domination, and I have fought against black domination. I have cherished the ideal of a democratic and free society in which all persons live together in harmony and with equal opportunities. It is an intent which I hope to live for and achieve. But if need be, it is an ideal for which I am prepared to die." Yet, he died in peace with his family at a good old age. And do you know what? It is said that during those twenty-seven years he spent in prison, he ran in place in his cell the equivalent of seven miles every day!

Nelson Mandela
1918–2013

"Not by might, nor by power, but by my spirit, saith the Lord of hosts." (Zechariah 4:6)

34

STUBBORN WINNER

The 1920s, West Virginia

Father came home from his carpenter shop with a big picture.

"See what I found! I stopped to see what was left over from the auction down the street, and there was this big picture of the Ten Commandments!"

The family gathered around, and one of them said, "Oh, look, each commandment has a picture with it!"

Little Desmond pointed to a picture next to one of the commandments. "What's this one with a man with a club?"

Father fingered his beard. "Why, that's Cain. That's his brother, Abel, lying there. Cain has just killed him."

"Why did he kill his brother?" Desmond looked into his father's face. "Why would anybody want to kill his brother?"

"I don't know, Son, maybe jealousy. To explain it would be to excuse it."

Desmond turned to his brother. "I would never want to do that to you, no matter what."

His brother reached out his hand, and they touched fingers.

"And I'm not ever going to kill anybody!" Desmond announced.

He didn't know then what trouble that resolve would cause him in the future.

When World War II broke out, Desmond said, "I need to do my part for my country." He enlisted in the army. There his commitment never to kill came under serious condemnation along with his faith in God. When his officers insisted he carry a gun, he replied, "No, I can't do that." Angry that they couldn't make him obey, they tried to court martial him. They even tried to declare him mentally incapable of serving in the military, but he refused to back down. The men in his unit made fun of him, throwing their boots at him when he knelt by his bed for his evening prayers. One of the men would say in a baby voice, "Now I lay me down to sleep." But he just ignored them and went to sleep.

Finally, he was assigned to work in the medical unit. He bathed and bandaged march-worn, blistered feet, which could have been caused by some of the boots that had been thrown at him. He was sent along with his division to Guam and the Philippines where he rescued under fire the injured and cared for them. On the island of Okinawa, where the enemy secretly planned to attack the Americans when they all reached the top of a plateau by opening fire on them from hidden caves and trenches, many American soldiers were killed or badly injured. Desmond went up and began pulling the wounded to the edge of the 400-foot cliff, pulling them one by one behind him on a stretcher, then tying them securely with a double bowline knot that he had learned in his Pathfinder club back home, and lowering them down a steep embankment. With bullets whizzing by, Desmond would pray, "Just one more, Lord, help me save one more!" With that faith and determination, he rescued more than 75 men.

> *"Just one more, Lord, help me save one more!"*

Another day, he was severely wounded himself and lost his pocket Bible on the battlefield. The men, who now respected his faith and commitment, went out after the battle was over, found the Bible, and brought it back to him.

After the war, he was awarded the first Medal of Honor ever given to a conscientious objector.

Desmond Doss
1919–2006

Jesus taught—*"Love your enemies, bless them that curse you, do good to them that hate you, and pray for them which despitefully use you, and persecute you; that ye may be the children of your Father which is in heaven ..."* (Matthew 5:44, 45)

35

THE CLAUSTROPHILE

1932, Brooklyn, New York

The candy store smelled so good—like the delicious fudge cooking in the back room. Father, a Jewish businessman from Russia, waited on customers out front, displaying all kinds of colorfully decorated sweet things: peppermint, licorice, strawberry, vanilla, chocolate—all carefully arranged under glass. Mother, in charge of making the candy, put all three children to work as soon as they got home from school. What a wonderful way to make a living!

Twelve-year-old Isaac liked to work out front with his father, making friends with customers, wrapping their goodies carefully in white boxes and tissue, and attaching a ribbon bow on each. When things quieted down, he would take a magazine from the newspaper and magazine rack and read. He loved to read. He had taught himself to read at age five, and having all those articles and stories close at hand gave him his greatest pleasure. He could never have bought that much reading material.

"Dad," he said one day, "I'm so glad there's a lot to learn right here in our shop."

"Well, I'm glad you're glad, Son, as long as you pay attention to what needs to be done here. You seem to be keeping up with your duties here, and your grades at school are good. So, go ahead, have at it. I'll let you know if you need to speed up on extra work."

"Dad," Isaac said a little later as he settled down to read again, "You know what kind of a job I'd really like to have?"

"What, Son?"

"You know those little sheds down in the subway where newspapers are sold to passengers?"

"Yes."

"That's what I'd like to do!"

"But it's dark down there except for inside the sheds, and they're so small. And you couldn't get out unless a train stopped for you."

"I would love it! I could read and read and write …"

"Well, I think you'd better stay where you are."

Isaac didn't work in any little sheds, but he often went by himself to some small place to read and write. He graduated from high school at age fifteen.

In college, Isaac took a major in zoology, but when they started dissecting cats, he said to himself, "These are perfectly good healthy cats. Why would anybody want to kill them and cut them into pieces? Isn't there some easier way to teach?" Apparently, there wasn't, so he changed his major to chemistry. He graduated with a Bachelor of Science degree at age nineteen. Eventually he became a professor of biochemistry at Boston University. In the meantime, he read voraciously everything he could get his hands on. And he wrote, wrote, and wrote some more!

He wrote clear explanations of all kinds of subjects, almost all the categories found in the library (nine out of the ten categories in the Dewey Decimal Classification system): history of physics, chemistry, astronomy, mathematics, history of Greece, Rome, Egypt, the near East, and the *Chronology of the World*. *Asimov's Guide to the Bible* includes the history of each book, a survey of the political influences, and the background of the characters in both the Old and New Testaments. He was best known for his books on science fiction. He became a popular speaker to audiences everywhere because he could make them understand hard subjects.

Isaac Asimov is credited with having originated 600 books, games, audio recordings, videos, and wall charts, besides an estimated 90,000 letters and postcards in which he answered questions from his readers! His one cardinal rule in writing was "BE CLEAR." And, as someone said, "He can make your mouth water over the driest subjects." And where do you think he wrote most of those masterful works at 90 words per minute on his electric typewriter? In a claustrophile's haven—his attic.

Isaac Asimov
1920–1992

"For it is God which worketh in you both to will and to do of his good pleasure." (Philippians 2:13)

36

I HAVE A DREAM

1936, Atlanta, Georgia

"But Mother, why can't I play with him? He likes me ... and I like him. We have so much fun together!" asked Martin with tears filling his eyes.

"I know, dear," said Mother, looking over at Father. Their eyes met and silently they agreed it was time to explain some things to their seven-year-old.

Father sat down on the sofa and drew his son on his lap. "You see, Son, not many things in this world are as they should be. Yes, the world of nature is constant, the sun comes up every morning, and the birds and blossoms come back in the spring. But human beings are not that way. The old devil puts hate into people sometimes, and they become cruel and cause fighting and wars. Most of the white people around here don't like us dark-skinned people. We were brought here from Africa where everyone is black. God made other people with different colored skin—red American Indians, yellow Chinese, very white Norwegians, tan Italians—and He loves them all."

"His dad said he can't play with me anymore."

Martin looked into his father's face.

"Well, that's the way it is. You remember that there are white schools and black schools in this city."

"But Dad, it's not right!"

"Well, the whites don't want us around because they think we are ignorant and dirty and that they are better."

Mother got up from her chair and said, "Someday things will get better. We just have to be patient, do what's right, and wait."

And wait they did. Public eating places, water fountains, restrooms, city parks, and museums did not welcome blacks. If blacks broke the rules, the police came and arrested them. Blacks were not allowed to live in white neighborhoods.

When Martin was seventeen, he entered a speech contest in another city. Because he was so well-read and well-spoken and because everybody liked him for his friendliness and courtesy, they sent him to the state contest. His subject was "The Negro and the Constitution," for which he won second prize.

"I'm so proud of you!" said his teacher as they boarded the bus for home. They sat in the back where the blacks were supposed to sit, but as the bus filled up and more white folks got on, the bus driver shouted, "You Negroes get up and let these folks have your seats!" Martin and his teacher were gathering up their bags when the driver shouted again with cursing and swearing. As the two of them stood most of the way home, Martin became angry in his heart and thought to himself, *Fine thing! What's the good of my making a speech about equality in the Constitution when things like this happen every day!* But finally, the day came when a black worker named Rosa Parks refused to give up her seat on a city bus, was arrested, and landed in jail. As a result, the black community refused to ride the buses in that city for almost a year. Thousands of them walked to work. That began the great struggle for equality in the United States.

Martin, now grown up, spoke often to his people. "We can win in this battle if we use the method taught by Mahatma Gandhi. The people of India won their independence from England by peaceful means only, and that will be the secret of our success." The black community adopted that approach even though many suffered from violent attacks. Finally, with the help of the Federal Congress, the Supreme Court, and Presidents Kennedy and Johnson, federal laws were passed and enforced which gave the black people their Constitutional rights to learn, move about freely, and accomplish their goals of living honest, decent lives.

Martin Luther King, Jr. died at age 39 of a gunshot wound, but had fulfilled his calling. His dream came true even though today some hate other races. Here is one of the lessons he taught:

"Your self-image should not come from the job you do but from how well you do your job. If your job is sweeping streets, then you have to sweep them as good as Leonardo da Vinci painted, Beethoven wrote music, and Longfellow wrote poetry."

Martin Luther King, Jr.
1929–1968

> *"In God have I put my trust: I will not be afraid what man can do unto me. ... They have prepared a net for my steps; my soul is bowed down: they have digged a pit before me, into the midst whereof they are fallen themselves."* (Psalms 56:11; 57:6)

37

THE GIANT STEP FOR MANKIND

1945, Ohio

The door to the doughnut shop opened with a ding and shut as a teen-age boy entered. "Is my buddy here?"

The baker pointed toward the back. "He's in the dough mixer."

"Where?"

"Go back and see."

Sure enough, there was Neil down inside the big mixer. "Hey, Bud, what are you doing down in there? You'll turn into a doughnut!"

"Nah, I'm cleaning it out. Everybody here is too big to get inside."

"Well, OK, I just came in to see if you want to play ball with the guys."

"No, when I get done here I have to mow out at the cemetery."

"Aw, you're a glutton for punishment!"

"Not really," said Neil as he climbed out of the mixer, pieces of dough sticking to his baker's clothing. "I've got a flying lesson tomorrow that I have to pay for."

Neil had wanted to fly since his first plane ride at age six. His dad, an Ohio state auditor, had encouraged him but said that he must pay for the lessons himself. His stay-at-home mother and his Sunday School teacher patiently watched him read books (he had read 100 books when he was in first grade) and occasionally bought him aviation magazines which he eagerly devoured. He drew pictures and built paper models with his Boy Scout friends. As it turned out, Neil earned his pilot's license on his sixteenth birthday—before he got his driver's license!

He also went to college, joined the Navy Airforce, flew fighter jets in the Korean War, escaped death by parachuting into water after being hit by enemy anti-aircraft guns, and studied aeronautical engineering. Later he flew a rocket-propelled X-15 at 4,000 miles per hour and reached the altitude of 207,500 feet (40 miles up). Most commercial airlines go 600 miles per hour at an altitude of 40,000 feet.

Neil married and had three children. The youngest, a little girl whom he adored, was stricken with cancer and died at age three. He dealt with his overwhelming sorrow by setting a new goal—he applied to become an astronaut. That meant more study, practice, and progress. In 1969, he became the first man to walk on the moon. His famous words went around the world, "One small step for a man and one giant leap for mankind."

From doughnut mixer to space capsule, Neil Armstrong, aeronautical engineer, naval aviator, test pilot, astronaut, and later university professor, the Boy Scout who mowed grass on the earth to learn to fly and who went to the moon, set an example for any boy in any country or culture. Think of your possibilities!

Neil Armstrong

1930-2012

"For the Lord of hosts hath purposed and who shall disannul it? And his hand is stretched out, and who shalt turn it back?" (Isaiah 14:27)

38

BELOVED SOLDIER

1955, New York City

Eighteen-year-old Colin burst through the front door of his home in South Bronx, New York, after classes at City College. The crisp October air fanned the fabric on his mother's sewing machine where she made clothing for her customers, and the fragrance of dinner told him she was in the kitchen. In fact, Father, a shipping clerk, was there too. Both of them were Jamaican with a little Scottish blood mixed in.

"Mom! Dad! I got it! Man, I got it!"

"Got what?" Dad laid his newspaper down on the table. Mother turned down the burner on the stove and came over too.

Colin paced the floor in excitement. "You know how I never could decide what I wanted to be when I grew up?"

Father laughed. "Yeah, I'm forty and still don't know what I'm going to be when I grow up."

Mother wiped her hands on her apron. "So what happened, Son?"

"Well, they've got this special course at school called the ROTC."

"ROTC, what's that?"

"That's Reserve Officer's Training Corps."

Father shifted his chair a bit. "Officers of what?"

"Of the army!" Colin's face took on a look of pride.

Mother turned toward the stove again. "Oh, Colin, the army? We've had so much war!"

"You know it's dangerous business, Son." Father looked away.

"Oh, yes!" Colin sat down at the table. "But what they need is good leadership. I love the order and discipline. I love the camaraderie!"

Mother set the dinner on the table. "Well, some of those army people are less than good friend material."

"But, Mom, you find that everywhere you go."

"Well, Son," Dad said. "Let's pray about it." And they did, right there at the dinner table.

Colin went on to become a leader in his unit. His career gave him structure and direction, which led him not only into danger but it also gave him the opportunity to train his men, even rescuing them in spite of being wounded himself. He received many military medals including the Purple Heart and the Bronze Star. He became a Four-Star General and was appointed Chief Military Strategist during Desert Storm and Chairman of the Joint Chiefs of Staff. Later he was the first black American to become Secretary of State.

Since retirement he has devoted himself to public speaking and motivating young people and adults to achieve better personal management and health. Here are two of the principles he teaches:

- A dream doesn't become reality through magic; it takes sweat, determination, and hard work.
- If you are going to achieve excellence in big things, you must develop the habit in little matters. Excellence is not an exception; it is a prevailing attitude.

Colin Powell
1937–

"Endure hardness, as a good soldier of Jesus Christ. No man that warreth entangleth himself with the affairs of this life; that he may please him who hath chosen him to be a soldier." (2 Timothy 2:3, 4)

39

CLEAN AND STRAIGHT

1958, Baltimore, Maryland

"Oh, no!" cried the children as they neared home after school. "Our furniture is out on the street again!"

Mother had gotten behind on her rent again, and this was the third time they had been evicted. But she was determined to keep her eight children in church school even if she found herself in trouble—like now.

"Don't you kids worry," she said as she arrived home from her work as a domestic. "We'll get somebody to come with a truck, and all of you will help load. Things are going to get better. 'All things work together for good to them that love the Lord …'"

Ten-year-old Barry finished the Bible verse in his mind, "… *and are called according to his purpose." Is this going to turn out good, or are we always going to live in these kinds of city ghettos with prostitutes and drug dealers on every corner?*

Dad wasn't much help. A long-distance truck driver, he seldom came home, and, when he did, he would drink himself into a stupor and become violent. Mother did her best to teach the children. One evening as they sat at the supper table, she announced, "You need to start memorizing Bible verses. The ones you memorize while you are young will always stay with you. I am offering five cents to you for every Bible verse you memorize."

"Wow!" they all shouted. "Thanks, Mom!" and off they went to earn nickels.

One day, Barry found a passage that changed his life: 1 Peter 1:18, 19.

"Forasmuch as ye know that ye were not redeemed with corruptible things, as silver and gold, from your vain conversation [useless living] received by tradition from your fathers, but with the precious blood of Christ, as of a lamb without blemish and without spot."

Barry thought, *The price of an item is based on what people are willing to pay for it. Now, if God has bought me back from a useless life, and He didn't use money but sent His Son to die for me, that must mean that I am very important to Him.* "For God so loved the world, that He gave His only begotten Son, that whosoever believeth in him should not perish, but have everlasting life" (John 3:16). *That means that I don't have to feel hurt when somebody looks down their nose at me. I'm valuable! God is my father; He's called me, and I'm going to live for Him!*

And he did. Along with his seven siblings, he finished school, prayed much, and worked his way through private college and graduate school. He continued his studies in several universities, earned three masters' degrees and two doctoral degrees. He joined the United States Navy where he became a Navy Chaplain. He received many awards and medals while serving at home and overseas. Rear Admiral Barry Black became Chief of Navy Chaplains.

After 27 years, he retired from the Navy and became the 62nd Chaplain of the United States Senate. He was the first black man and the first Seventh-day Adventist to serve in that office, teaching and encouraging government leaders to do their best to keep their integrity in spite of opposition and difficult world affairs.

He says to everyone, especially young people, "Isolate yourself for greatness."

Barry Black
1948–

"He which soweth sparingly shall reap also sparingly, and he which soweth bountifully shall reap also bountifully. Every man according as he purposeth in his heart, so let him give; not grudgingly, or of necessity; for God loveth a cheerful giver. And God is able to make all grace abound toward you; that ye, always having all sufficiency in all things, may abound to every good work." (2 Corinthians 9:6–8)

40

CONVERSION IN A BATHROOM

1964, Detroit, Michigan

The teacher held up a black stone. "Who can tell me what kind of stone this is?"

Silence reigned in the schoolroom. Every face looked blank. Slowly a hand went up—Benny, the class dunce. Somebody snickered.

"Benny!" the teacher said, "Do you know?"

"It's obsidian. It's formed by lava cooling fast, and it's called natural glass."

"That's right!"

The teacher looked surprised as did the other students. They looked at each other, then at Benny. He had never come up with an answer—any answer. He was the dumbest kid in class. How could this be?

"Benny, I want to see you in my office after school."

Benny's face fell. He gulped. Not again! He couldn't tell what he'd done wrong this time.

After school he slinked into the teacher's office. But the teacher greeted him with a warm smile.

"Benny, how did you know about obsidian? What's happened to you?"

Benny relaxed; he wasn't in trouble after all. "Well, I've been reading this book about rocks from the library."

"Library? You've been to the library?"

"Yeah, my mom has said we can watch TV only a couple hours a week. And we have to read two books a week and write her a report on each one. At first, my brother and I didn't like it a bit, but I've gotten so I enjoy it. I'm learning all kinds of exciting things."

"Well, that's excellent, Benny," replied the teacher. "You know, I've got an idea. Come over to this lab table. I want to show you something."

What the teacher had was a microscope, and when Benny peered into it, his whole world changed. Small things turned into big things. And what he thought was big wasn't big at all! He thought about that a few years later when he turned 14. As a result of his reading and writing reports, he had rocketed to the head of his class and his school.

I'm going to the top, he thought to himself, *I can be anything I want to be. Mother is right. Nothing is going to stop me. I'm going to be an important guy. I'm already important!* But a few weeks later, he ran through the bathroom door at home, slammed it shut, locked it, and collapsed on the floor.

"Oh, God, how could I do such a thing?" The picture in his mind repeated itself for the umpteenth time as he ran home. Nobody was there. He closed his eyes. He sobbed until he couldn't cry any more.

He had lost his temper at something his friend had said, and Ben had stabbed him with his pocketknife. But the knife blade had broken against his friend's belt buckle and had fallen to the ground.

"I almost killed him—I lost my temper, Lord. What am I going to do? Mom taught me to stay close to You, but I haven't done that. Lord, what am I going to do? Can You hear me? Please. Why do I get so mad? You saw me start to hit her the other day when she said she couldn't buy me designer clothes, and I would've if Brother hadn't stopped me. I think You had him there so she would be protected.

"And come to think of it, You had my friend wear his belt with the big buckle today. You were protecting him—and me too! Oh, Father God, please take away this bad temper. I'll do everything I can to control myself, but I can't do it by myself. Please help me!"

And God did. Ben learned that he wasn't as big and important as he had thought. He became a real student, calm and quiet, through high school, college, and medical school by reading, reading, and reading. Finally, Ben Carson, African American and Seventh-day Adventist, became a world-famous neurosurgeon, and later he became a member of the Cabinet of President of the United States Donald Trump.

Ben Carson

1951–

"He that is slow to anger is better than the mighty; and he that ruleth his spirit than he that taketh a city." (Proverbs 16:32)

"Come unto me, all ye that labor and are heavy laden, and I will give you rest. Take my yoke upon you, and learn of me; for I am meek and lowly in heart: and ye shall find rest unto your souls. For my yoke is easy, and my burden is light." (Matthew 11:28–30)

41

DO IT RIGHT!

1968, Seattle, Washington

Four sets of parents waited in the principal's office looking at each other with questioning eyes. A "guest" was to be arriving soon.

One said, "Well, our sons are all best friends, and they're all good students. I can't imagine any trouble they could've gotten into."

"Who knows?" replied another, "The world is getting crazier every day."

A mother gazed at the United States president's picture on the wall, "But they're all so smart."

The door opened, and two men entered, but before it closed, the four boys could be seen sitting nervously in the waiting room. "This is Mr. ___, president of Computer Center Company," said the principal, as he introduced each of the parents who stood and greeted the guest with handshakes and questioning smiles.

After everyone was seated, the principal continued, "You mothers, members of the Mothers' Club, all worked so hard to raise money to buy our school's teletype machine that is connected to Computer Center Company's big computer so our students could learn this new technology. You have also provided money so computer time could be purchased for them. This is a way for our students to make their way in the scientific world, and I want to personally thank you."

One of the mothers said, "But we're sorry—we've run out of money. Now the students must come up with their own money to buy computer time."

"That has to do with why we're here tonight." He turned to the president. "Will you share your thoughts with us now?"

The company president leaned forward.

"You folks are certainly aware that your sons are foremost in learning computer technology. In fact, let me say, they have proven that their skills exceed some of the best minds in our company." He leaned back in his chair. "In fact, your boys have found some glitches in our system and have offered to share their findings with us if we give them free computer time—which we agreed to—for a time." He leaned forward again with his elbows on his lap and his hands clasped together. "I wouldn't go so far as to say it's dishonesty, but young folks nowadays are so quick to take advantage …"

So, the parents all agreed to a three-month ban during summer vacation on their sons' computer privileges. When the boys came in and heard the story, they accepted the decision. When the three-month ban was over and school had started again, the company hired them, and they earned their computer time along with some income. One of them, Bill, wrote his first program, a computer game of tic-tac-toe, when he had just turned thirteen. From then on, computers became his first love. He had always been a reader; in fact, he read the entire set of *World Book Encyclopedias* when he was seven years old. His habit of being hard on himself paid off. He became the inventor, along with his school friend Paul, of a small computer. From huge computers that took up the space of a large room to the small laptops of today with much greater speed and capability, Bill was at the center of the development of the software that runs them.

Today, Bill invests his huge fortune in helping improve the health, education, and chances for improvement for millions of the world's population.

There are thousands of pieces of information regarding the life of Bill Gates that we don't have room for here, but one thing we know—God gifted him and called him to improve computer technology with a special determination to learn and work hard. Bill says, "It's fine to celebrate success, but it's more important to heed the lessons of failure."

Bill Gates
1955–

"I will very gladly spend and be spent for you." (2 Corinthians 12:15)

TEACH Services, Inc.
PUBLISHING
www.TEACHServices.com • (800) 367-1844

We invite you to view the complete
selection of titles we publish at:
www.TEACHServices.com

We encourage you to write us
with your thoughts about this,
or any other book we publish at:
info@TEACHServices.com

TEACH Services' titles may be purchased in
bulk quantities for educational, fund-raising,
business, or promotional use.
bulksales@TEACHServices.com

Finally, if you are interested in seeing
your own book in print, please contact us at:
publishing@TEACHServices.com

We are happy to review your manuscript at no charge.

www.ingramcontent.com/pod-product-compliance
Lightning Source LLC
Chambersburg PA
CBHW050929240426
43671CB00019B/2961